The Life and Times of Falkirk

The Life and Times of Falkirk

IAN SCOTT

JOHN DONALD PUBLISHERS LTD
EDINBURGH

Reprinted 1995

ISBN 0 85976 386 2
British Library Cataloguing in Publication Data
A catalogue record for this book is available from the
British Library.

Phototypeset by ROM-Data Corporation Ltd, Falmouth,
Cornwall.
Printed & bound in Great Britain by Bell & Bain Ltd., Glasgow.

Preface

In the twenty years since Lewis Lawson's excellent History of
Falkirk was published by the old Town Council there has been a
tremendous increase in interest in the history of the town and its
surrounding district. A great deal of new research has added to
our knowledge and understanding of the centuries from the time
of the Roman occupation to the present day - from the Legions to
the Regions as one wit has it. My intention here is to describe the
life and times of Falkirk by drawing on recent research as well as
the accumulated wisdom of the many antiquarians and local historians who have left us such a fine legacy. And what a story it is! It
is doubtful if any other town in Scotland can claim such a fascinating range of historical experience - the Antonine Wall and the two
canals, the mighty iron furnaces of Carron, two great battles, unruly
feudal barons, the huge cattle trysts of the 19th century, Victorian
prosperity brought by over thirty iron foundries and, appropriately
enough, the birthplace of Irn Bru!

Many people have contributed to the telling of this story, not
least my friends and colleagues in Falkirk Local History Society. In
particular I must record my special thanks to John Reid and Geoff
Bailey whose researches over the last decade have added so much
to our knowledge of everything from the feudal parishes to the
aerated water trade, including such diverse topics as place names,
the Roman occupation, the Cromwellian and Jacobite periods and
the stentmasters of the town. They have been involved at every
stage of the preparation of this book and if the words are mine,
the brightest ideas are theirs without a doubt. They have also
contributed several maps and drawings for which I am very grateful.
John Walker was good enough to read through the final manuscript and I am grateful for his advice and assistance. I would also
like to thank Marion Fenwick and Dorothy Erskine who typed the
manuscript, and Russell Walker of John Donald Ltd., who was most
helpful at all stages of the production. My wife Irene has been

living with my addiction to the history of this wonderful place for so many years now that she is almost as involved as I am. Nonetheless I thank her here for unlimited patience when I wandered off yet again in pursuit of a book or a picture or a pint in the Wheatsheaf!

Inevitably there will be things in this book which some readers will dispute - I hope there are, for argument and discussion are the most enjoyable parts of the whole historical scene! I apologise in advance to those who are disappointed at missed topics, or with the slight treatment given to their favourite place or theme. Each village in the district deserves its own book and many aspects must wait for another time and place. Despite this I hope that this account helps to stimulate an interest in Falkirk and its surroundings, especially among the younger generation who are the makers of the future.

Falkirk, 1994   I. S.

Acknowledgements

The front-cover illustration is from a painting by William Aitken, D.A., of Falkirk High Street in 1957. It is reproduced here by kind permission of Mr R. Wilson, F.R.I.A.S.

The photograph of Callendar House on the back cover is by Allan Meek, and is used without his kind permission — but he'll no mind!

Photographs within the text, unless otherwise stated, are from contemporary sources or are by the author.

Contents

CHAPTER 1

The Legions of Rome

The town of Falkirk stands in the very heart of Central Scotland at the point where the southern uplands slope gently down to the valley of the River Forth. Although the flat and fertile carse lands to the north and east, and the pasturage and mineral wealth of the higher ground behind the town to the south, brought relative prosperity to the area over the centuries, it was Falkirk's position overlooking the river which ensured its central role in Scotland's story from the very earliest times. For centuries the Forth proved a formidable barrier to movement and all the major land routes from south to north, or east to west between the castle towns of Edinburgh and Stirling, crossed the Falkirk district. And it was to the river estuary that the first people came to live and work in the centuries after the ice disappeared over ten thousand years ago.

Who they were, where they came from or exactly when, remain as yet unknown, and only tantalising fragments of their story, accidentally uncovered over the last century or so, confirm their existence in this part of central Scotland. Earliest and most spectacular of all are the great 'middens'—mountains of shells discarded by a people who hugged the beaches of the firth for centuries before the art of tillage and husbandry freed them from their dependance on the sea. At Nether Kinneil, in 1978 archaeologists discovered one such enormous stone age deposit—fifteen tons of oyster shells—discarded at various dates ranging from 2500 to 4000 BC. Elsewhere at nearby Polmonthill and Inveravon, on beaches once at sea level and now many feet above the river, similar mounds speak of neolithic man spreading along the Forth, using bone and stone implements to hunt and fish and finally to practice rudimentary agriculture on fertile clearings in the great forests which cloaked much of the land area here for tens of centuries.

A thousand years after the shell middens were abandoned another scattering of relics confirms the existence of men of the 'bronze' age. At Camelon, stone kist burials containing food vessels

1

from 1500 BC or thereabouts, along with cremated remains and flint tools; at Stenhousemuir, in the Goshen sands, a bronze spear head close to another kist; and most amazing of all, at Denny a long bow made of oak dated at 1200 BC, one of five such weapons found in Britain and the only one made of this material found in Europe. Inflexible oak certainly seems an unlikely choice for a longbow even in Denny, and one is left to speculate on how long the bow maker remained in this particular business before moving on to a more profitable enterprise! In other parts of the district settlements from a century or so later have been found, with evidence of defensive palisades protecting houses with cooking pits—the homes of farmers of the late bronze and early iron age—around 500-100 BC.

Fascinating as these discoveries are, they represent no more than a handful of pieces in a puzzle of almost infinite size. There is very little continuity in the snapshot pictures they provide of peoples separated by many centuries from each other and from us, and much more awaits discovery. More systematic excavation is required, but little is happening at present and the task of completing the picture must remain for future generations.

We can be fairly sure however that over many centuries, several waves of settlers found their way from the continent to this part of the country, eventually merging with or superseding earlier arrivals and ultimately living in loose tribal groupings with similar language and traditions. They were the ancestors of those whom later generations would call the Picts and who were the first to encounter the formidable Legions of the Roman Emperor towards the end of the first century A.D. And it is only with the arrival of the Romans in Scotland that we can talk with any certainty about the early history of Falkirk district and even begin to speculate on the origins of the town itself.

In the year 80 AD the Governor of Britain, Julius Agricola, pushed northwards in an attempt to secure the southern territories of Britannia by subduing the hostile tribes. Possession of the central valley was obviously crucial to such an undertaking and number of small fortlets were built across the country as well as roads both north and south of the line. At Camelon a heavily garrisoned fort guarded the vital crossing point of the River Carron, and from this base Agricola conducted a number of punitive campaigns against the northern tribes culminating in the great Roman victory of

Mons Graupius somewhere in the north east. Despite this success, opposition to the Roman presence continued to grow and after more than a decade of sustained pressure the legions began a gradual withdrawal from central Scotland. By AD 100 they were once again on the line of Solway and Tyne.

It was forty years before the Romans returned to the district and it was possibly during this absence that local tribesmen of whom we know very little, constructed the formidable defensive position, at Torwood, a mile or so north of the Carron crossing. This mighty circular stone broch of Tappoch stood on high ground not far from Agricola's north road and may have been over 20 feet high with walls of the same thickness enclosing an area over 30 feet in diameter. The walls contained rooms, passages and stairs and the whole was probably designed as an occasional safe retreat for the tribesmen and their families in times of difficulty. The existence of such a defensive structure in this part of Scotland far from the traditional broch area of the north west, has exercised the minds of scholars over the years with some suggesting the existence of itinerant broch builders selling their skills well beyond their normal domain, while others see Tappoch as the work of immigrants drawn south in the era after Agricola's departure. More recently it has been argued that many similar structures may have been in use during the early iron age but that they have been lost or wrongly identified in succeeding ages. Whatever its origin the broch remains an amazing structure despite the deterioration wrought by our own careless age and it can still be seen by visitors to the Torwood area. From the vantage point afforded by the high stone rampart the inhabitants must have watched in dismay as the feared legionary eagles signalled the return of the formidable Roman fighting machine to the district in 139 AD.

Despite the construction of the mighty Hadrian's Wall in northern England in 128 AD the Romans came north once again in what must have been another attempt to subdue their troublesome neighbours. It is with this advance under Lollius Urbicus that the real story of Roman Falkirk begins. In 142 AD Agricola's abandoned posts were replaced by the great 38 mile wall from Forth to Clyde everywhere dedicated to the Roman Emperor Antoninus Pius and known to our age as the Antonine Wall. Fifteen miles of this incredible work of engineering lie in Falkirk district, from the starting point on the Forth near Bo'ness, through the very centre

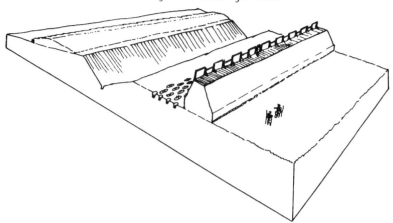

An impression of a section of the Antonine Wall showing the turf rampart, the defensive ditch and the lillia to the north. *Drawing* Geoff Bailey.

of the town itself and on past Bonnybridge and Castlecary to the west. Though not so long, high, or permanent as the stone barrier of Hadrian, it was by any standard an amazing achievement involving the combined energies of detachments from at least four legions, perhaps 10,000 men in all, over a period of nearly two years.

The builders began by laying a six to nine inch thick base of stone some fifteen feet wide with squared or 'dressed' stones along the outside edges and unshaped stone rubble in the middle. At intervals along the length of this base they left stone-lined drainage culverts. Upon this solid bed stood the great rampart of the wall itself rising ten feet and tapering from fourteen to six feet in width at the top where a wooden palisade or breast work increased the height by another four or five feet. The wall was built according to a familiar Roman pattern using blocks of turf rather than stone and, in an apparent attempt to compensate for its relative fragility, the Roman engineers placed an even bigger ditch to the north than had been the case at Hadrians. Varying between thirty and forty feet wide in places and up to fifteen feet deep this great V-shaped barrier lay some twenty or thirty feet from the base of the wall and, though it was never planned as a moat, the drainage culverts, Caledonian weather and sewage from the forts where up to twenty thousand men were eventually garrisoned ensured that it was seldom empty in the winter months! In front of the ditch the

The surviving ditch at Watling Lodge in Camelon.

excavated earth was, in most places, thrown up to create yet another obstacle helping to complete what must have seemed to the watching tribesmen in their hill forts and brochs an utterly impregnable barrier, towering above the flat lands of the river valley and stretching in a continuous line both east and west as far as the eye could see.

It was a silent but constant reminder of the sheer power of the Roman invaders, intended to impress and overawe the local tribes But, as has often happened before and since, mighty power goes down in the dust of the centuries. Hardly a trace of the rampart now remains anywhere, though the great ditch can be identified here and there either from surface markings or as a genuine depression often up to 15 feet deep. In Callendar Park for example, a fine stretch is quite evident, and at Watling Lodge in Camelon, visitors can come closest to experiencing the ditch as it was eighteen hundred years ago. Forty feet wide and fifteen feet deep, it is the best preserved example on the whole length of the wall. Between these two points to the east and west of the town, the line of ditch and wall has been plotted with as much accuracy as occasional excavation will allow. From Callendar Park it ran across modern Kemper Avenue towards the Pleasance, across Cockburn Street, Arnothill and Maggie Woods Loan to Frobisher Avenue, Blinkbonny Road and on towards Watling Lodge. Approximately twenty feet behind the wall to the south ran the continuous line of the military way, a substantial service road designed to allow rapid movement of troops to reinforce any part of the wall. The whole mighty work and the construction of the roads, forts and fortlets which completed the defensive system was accomplished by professional soldiers from Rome and auxilliary troops recruited in various parts of the Emperor's huge domains. Detachments or 'vexillations' of four legions were involved—the second (Augusta), Sixth (Victrix), Twentieth (Valeria Victrix) and Twenty-second (Primigenia). Within their ranks were skilled surveyors and masons, woodcutters and road engineers and they were probably assisted by the pressed, paid or voluntary labour of the local inhabitants. Over the years twenty magnificent distance slabs have been discovered, on the whole length of the wall, which identify the builders and their particular contributions. Unfortunately only one of these refers to the Falkirk end of the wall but the compensation is that it is the most magnificent. This 'Bridgeness' slab discovered in 1868 near Bo'ness shows sculpted Roman figures on horseback with defeated tribesmen falling beneath flying hooves on one side, and on the other a ceremonial sacrifice seeking divine blessing on some great activity—a campaign perhaps or a mighty undertaking like the wall itself. The legend tells us that:

> For the Emperor Titus Aelius Hadrianus Antoninus Pius, Father of his country, the Second Augustan Legion completed the work for 4652 paces.

Many more such slabs await discovery—perhaps another forty may well lie hidden where the Romans buried them before the wall was finally abandoned—no doubt in time they will yield their secrets to future observers.

As well as the great rampart and the military way, the legionaries also built a series of forts and fortlets along the length of the wall to house the garrisons which would eventually hold the new frontier. Forts at Carriden near Bo'ness, Inveravon, Mumrills in Laurieston, Rough Castle and Castlecary have been identified and most excavated, and the projected town centre fort in Falkirk was confirmed by excavation in the Pleasance area in the late summer of 1991. Only Seabegs remains unlocated at the time of writing. In addition, small fortlets have been identified and excavated near

Seabegs, at Kinneil and most importantly at Watling Lodge in Camelon where the road north crossed the wall. A mile north of this fortlet the Romans built what must have been one of the most important forts in Scotland at Camelon.

Camelon's position was critical. To the east, the Forth itself provided a major barrier to movement towards the wall from the north If an attack was to come it would most likely funnel down through the natural gap between the Ochil and Lennox Hills in the valleys of the Forth and the Carron. The new Antonine fort at Camelon stood guard over this route and especially over the military road from the wall to the Carron and beyond, as had the original fort of Agricola sixty years earlier. Excavations in 1898 identified a complex maze of defensive ditches and building foundations which suggest several camps and forts of different periods and occupations. The Antonine fort alone occupied six acres of what is now Falkirk Golf Course and contained many substantial stone buildings capable of serving the needs of a very large garrison of soldiers.

Important as the site undoubtedly was it does seem a little over cautious to make such extensive provision for defence when the great wall half a mile south would provide even greater security, and this raises an interesting problem. It has always been the view of scholars that construction of the wall began near Bo'ness and proceeded by degrees across the country to the Clyde. But a glance at the map of Scotland shows that the stretch from Bo'ness to Camelon is something of a luxury since the Firth of Forth itself was surely barrier enough at the eastern end? And that stretch of wall is quite different in composition from the rest being built of clay and not turf blocks. Why should this be? Not because of a shortage of turf surely, for the eastern fortlet at Kinneil had turf ramparts. Could it be that the wall from Bo'ness to Falkirk was an afterthought, built when the Antonine frontier was complete? According to this theory, first proposed by archaeologist Geoff Bailey in 1991, the main work began not at Bo'ness but at Camelon with the fortlet of Watling Lodge and proceeded west using turf for the rampart. The gap between Watling Lodge and the River Forth, that is the eastern flank of the wall, was protected by the substantial fort at Camelon which would explain its size and importance. Later on, perhaps a year later, and for reasons that are not yet apparent, the additional section from Camelon to Bo'ness was completed, this time using clay. It is an intriguing thought and one that will no doubt fuel the never ending debate on this fascinating period in the history of the district.

The two forts on the wall nearest Falkirk offer a very interesting contrast of both size and function. The east end of Laurieston village, two miles from the town, shows no evidence today of its former glory, but where Sandyloan leaves the main street and bends round to Grahamsdyke Street, stood Mumrills, the biggest fort on the entire length of the wall, covering some six and a half acres. What a contrast the tranquillity of today's scene makes with bustling garrison of Tungrian cavalrymen from the Rhine and Thracian infantry from Bulgaria, perhaps 1000 in all, who occupied the substantial buildings that once stood here, protected on all sides by ramparts and ditches on the same scale as the wall itself. And what a contrast with the late 1920s when the legendary Sir George Macdonald and his team conducted extensive excavations over the whole site and established most of what we know today about Mumrills in AD 142.

Macdonald identified seven stone buildings including the head-quarters or 'principia' and a commanding officer's house or 'praetorium' with its own bathing area along with two granaries for storing the garrison food supply, and a bath house for the soldiers. Evidence of timber framed barrack buildings were also found and, along with many coins and pieces of pottery, two inscribed stones have been recovered in the locality telling something of the story of life and death among the Roman soldiers of the Mumrills garrison. One discovered near Brightons was an altar,

> sacred to Hercules Magusanus. Valerius Negrinus, Duplicarius of the Tungrian Cavalry Regiment was the dedicator.

and another, a tombstone dedicated to:

> The spirits of the departed. Nectovelus, son of Vindex, aged thirty, a Brigantian by tribe, he served for nine years the Second Cohort of Thracians.

The fort at Rough Castle two miles west of Falkirk was by contrast the second smallest on the wall and unlike Mumrills, one of the best preserved and presented. Again early excavation proved the

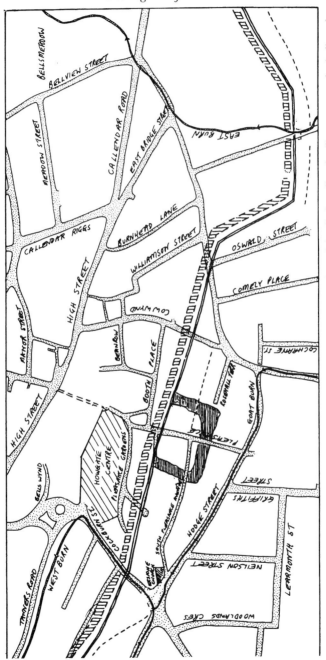

Falkirk town centre showing the locaton of the fort in the Pleasance area. The line of the ditch, wall and military way are also indicated. *Drawing Geoff Bailey.*

Falkirk archaeologist Geoff Bailey pictured during the excavation of the Falkirk
fort at Rosehall in the Pleasance area.

existence of the principia, praetoriam, granary and barracks, although the whole fort occupied just one acre. Like Mumrills there was an annexe, this time to the east of the fort, and here the foundations of a bathhouse have been identified. An inscribed tablet was discovered in the foundation of the headquarters building in 1903 identifying the builders of the Rough Castle fort as

> the sixth Cohert of the Nervii erected the principia for the Emperor Caesar Titus Aelius Hadrianus Antoninus Pius, Father of his Country

The Nervii who like the Tungrians were recruited by the Romans among the conquered peoples of the Rhine, were auxilliary troops who served alongside the Legion, Valeria Victrix which appears to have constructed this particular section of the wall with its forts and fortlets. The most interesting refinements added to the wall's defences here are the amazing ten rows of oval defensive pits once filled with sharp stakes camouflaged to resemble the surrounding land and called, with black Roman humour, the 'lilia' or lilies. It is common enough among observers these days to play down the Antonine Wall's role as a defensive position and suggest instead that it was no more than a frontier or even a customs barrier. It may, of course, have served as both but the lilies are a stark reminder that to the north of the wall lay an unknown number of 'Caledonian' tribesman who had already spent more than half a century fighting the invaders and would continue to do so with increasing vigour until the occupation of their territory was ended.

And what of the elusive fort of Falkirk itself? Midway between Mumrills and Rough Castle, the town centre had long been thought of as the likely site. Taking into account the established line of the wall and ditch in Callender Park and at several other points in the town, the area of the Pleasance—St Andrews Square and Booth Place—seemed the most likely place. Certainly the area had yielded a host of small finds over the years including coins, pottery, dressed and decorated stones all of which fit the period of the wall's occupation. Much of the area has been built over several times as the town expanded in the intervening centuries and the chances of locating the fort seemed to be diminishing with each passing generation. And yet, fresh discoveries are made from time to time, even in these days when mechanical power moves mountains and fills valleys with consummate ease and wipes out the traces of a hundred generations in one quiet afternoon. In the late summer of 1991 Geoff Bailey was able to confirm the Pleasance location when he excavated on the Rosehall site to the north of the Scout Hall and discovered the fort's defensive ditching along with Roman pottery of the Antonine period. At the time of writing further work is in progress, but we can be fairly certain that a substantial fort did stand on the area presently occupied by the Adrian Bowling Club. Jokes about 'Adrians Wall are being discouraged! This final confirmation of the fort's location followed another intriguing late discovery. In 1980 in a new car park in Kemper Avenue in the old 'Cleddens' area of the town, excavation identified the base of the wall and the foundation of an oblong building with a Roman hypocaust system, that is central heating channels. It seems to have been a Roman bathhouse and, though some distance from the probable fort, the crude nature of its construction suggests the possibility of local civilian use after the Roman period or perhaps an early entrepreneurial Falkirk 'bairn' providing a service for the soldiers of the garrison?

Were there local people settled in or near the forts? At Carriden

there is definite evidence of a 'vicus' or official civilian settlement
and there are many examples in Roman occupied territories of
tribes working with and for the legionaries, and enjoying the fruits
of the protection and relatively peaceful trading and working
conditions offered by this local 'pax Romana'. It seems very possible that such groups did exist in or near the Falkirk fort and it is
neither farfetched nor over romantic to see in such a 'vicus' the
first people of the town. We do not know who they were or what
they did or what they called their settlement, but when the Romans
left they may well have remained in place to begin the Falkirk story.
In 1933 an amazing hoard of Roman coins were discovered during
the excavation of the Callendar Riggs area, nearly 2000 in all,
covering several Imperial reigns. Such a collection, placed as it was
some distance in front of the wall and fort on the hostile northern
side, suggests hidden treasure probably accumulated from Roman
bribes by some tribal chief in return for securing local support.
Inside the urn which held the coins was a small piece of brown and
white checked crosswoven cloth. It is now a museum piece of
course, but it is still known as the 'Falkirk tartan' thought to be
earliest known example of the national weave in existence!

But before leaving Roman Falkirk one story remains to be told.
No aspect of the local occupation—walls, forts, ditches, tablets,
coins or weapons—has received quite so much attention over the
centuries as the incredible beehive shaped stone building which
for sixteen hundred years stood high up on the bank of the River
Carron some miles north of the wall. The story of this unique
building runs like a continuous thread through the many centuries
of its existence from its construction during the Roman occupation, through the dark age with its dubious links to the shadowy
legends of King Arthur, to the time of its wanton destruction in
1743. Arthur's O'on or Oven, as it was and still is known, stood
over twenty feet high and had a similar base diameter. The four
foot thick walls of dressed freestone narrowed towards the top
which was open when detailed architectural drawings were prepared in 1726. Described then as 'The Roman Sacellum of Mars
Signifier, vulgarly called Arthur's Oon' it was thought to be some
kind of temple or shrine—a brass finger from a long lost statue
found lodged inside the building seemed to confirm this view.
From its position out in the open, well in front of the wall, some
observers have argued that the O'on was a triumphal monument

An early drawing of Arthurs O'on which stood near the Stenhouse Mansion of
Sir Michael Bruce. He demolished it in 1743.

set up to further remind the Caledonians and other tribes of their
defeat and subjugation to the might of Rome. How it came to
acquire the Arthurian association is unclear, but by the sixteenth
century it was recognised by Scottish scholars as a Roman monument of considerable importance. This recognition, and the justifiable fame which the O'on enjoyed, did not preserve the
triumphal monument, perhaps the only one of its kind in Roman
Britain, from the fate which awaited it at the hand of Sir Michael
Bruce, Laird of Stenhouse, whose very estate and the village close
by—took their name from the great 'stone house' itself. In 1743
the Laird dismantled the building to provide a cheap supply of
dressed stones for a new weir on the River Carron. But the gods of
archaeology had the last word when a spate swept the ancient
stones away not long after the weir was built. When the scholars of
the day discovered this act of vandalism they did not spare Sir
Michael but prayed that 'if there is a pit deeper than ordinary
destined for the reception of such villains and sordid rascals,
condemn him to the bottom of it!' Another had an even more
painful fate in mind for Laird of Stenhouse:

In order to make his name execrable to all posterity, ...he should have an iron collar put about his neck like a yoke. At each extremity a stone of Arthur's O'on to be suspended... Thus accoutered let him wander on the banks of the Styx, perpetually agitated by angry demons with ox goads, 'Sir Michael Bruce' wrote on his back in large letters of burning phosphorus.

The passage of two and a half centuries has not modified the verdict or in any way rehabilitated the villain, whose act deprived future generations of such a special relic of the past, and one which would surely have delighted local people and drawn visitors from far and near. But though it is gone it is far from forgotten. Every year or so a new theory, as unlikely as its predecessor, seeks to place the O'on in a scheme linking various sites in Scotland with the dark age King Arthur and his famous knights. But these fanciful ideas vanish just as quickly as they appear only to return once again in a year or so. A much more interesting development came in the late 1980s when an American researcher Robert Mitchell claimed that the stones of the O'on were not scattered beneath the Carron waters at all but lay under a dismantled blast furnace where they were deposited when the river changed its course. He thus held up the possibility of recovery and reconstruction in the future, but so far there has been no confirmation of the find and no response to the proposal. Indeed the whole notion of the Carron having changed course at this point has been dismissed by other research-ers. John Reid of Falkirk who sees patterns in land forms that most other observers miss, has recently speculated that the O'on's posi-tion in relation to various key points on the Antonine Wall, as well as other prominent geographical features, suggests that it may have marked a fulcrum point in the mathematical calculations used by the Roman land surveyors to plan the construction of the whole barrier. A fascinating idea with plenty of persuasive geometrical evidence to support it, though not one taken up as yet by the 'official' wall watchers! As for the lost building itself, the interested observer can see a replica in Midlothian. So annoyed was the occupant of Penicuik House, Sir John Clerk, that he had his own O'on built in 1766 using the early drawings. It was used for many years as a doocot, perhaps the most unusual example in central Scotland. The site of the real O'on is now a housing estate, and no sign or mark tells a passer-by, or even the people who live there, of the former glory that lies beneath their feet. A sad finale indeed!

Despite such a triumphal monument and the seemingly impenetrable barrier behind it, the Roman stay in the district was remarkably short. The picture is very confused but it seems likely that the legions withdrew from the wall about 25 years after starting the building work and retired to the Hadrianic frontier. Sixty years later the aggressive campaigning of Septimus Severus brought the Romans back to Falkirk but it was a short lived occupation and by 210 AD the mighty wall with its network of roads and forts was finally abandoned and given over to the very tribes it was meant to subdue. What they did with the legacy is impossible to say, but the sheer scale of the barrier ensured that it loomed large in the lives of successive generations. They may have found that the road network offered a rapid east-west line of communication linking them with distant tribal groups. Alternatively the great wall and ditch may have restricted communications, separating peoples and defining territories for many centuries after the last Roman soldier departed for more hospitable climes.

CHAPTER 2

Christian Missioners and Feudal Barons

The eight centuries which follow the departure of the Romans from the Falkirk district present historians with an almost impossible task. Having dined on a rich harvest of archaeological evidence for the Roman occupation, they must now return to living of scraps carefully teased from a scattering of sources. Chronicles and annals, often recorded many centuries after the events, provide part of the story, but a careful analysis of place name evidence tells even more about the ebb and flow of competing cultures which struggled for supremacy in what was surely the birth crucible of the Scottish nation. Here the Pictish people beyond the Forth and Irish Scots from Argyll coalesced over the centuries with the Welsh speaking Britons of Strathclyde and the Germanic Angles pushing north through the Lothians.

Sometimes the conflicts which arose were resolved by clash of armies, and we are told by the chroniclers of great battles in Strathcarron or in the valley of the Forth between Pict and Angle, Scot and Briton by turns. The rivers ran red with blood so ferocious were the encounters and great destruction was wrought on both land and people. At such times the local population was no doubt elbowed aside and temporarily displaced by whatever invading army was active, but for the most part, the evidence such as it is, suggests a gradual change as the local inhabitants adapt to the ways of whatever new culture held sway at a particular period.

At some time during this period of migration and cultural evolution, and certainly before 1000 AD, Christian missionaries first arrived in the area, though who they were, when they came or who they met and taught, remains obscure. Some have even suggested that the Christian message came to the area with the Romans themselves in the last days of the occupation, but others look to the near mythical 'Saint Nynia', a Christian bishop from Roman Britain to the south. This St. Ninian first established a church at Candida Casa in Whithorn and, according to the

Venerable Bede writing three centuries later, went on to convert the 'southern picts' who probably occupied the territory just north of the Forth. Such a journey, along abandoned Roman roads and across the wall at Camelon, would have brought the missionary and his followers into the Falkirk area around 400 AD. Might they have chosen the gentle little hill just fifty yards or so in front of the wall, facing across the valley towards his chosen mission field, to site a little shrine or church? Or did those early inhabitants have to wait for the great mission of St. Columba, which radiated from Iona towards the end of the sixth century, for their first introduction to the Gospel message which would have such a profound influence on future generations? Oral tradition certainly supports this view, for the foundation of the church at Falkirk has for many centuries been associated with an early 7th or 8th century Celtic missionary called Mo-Aidan or Modan, probably the most famous of several who bear the name. This man, who is said to have 'tamed external senses of sight and hearing that he never experienced the irregular motions of sin', worked in Argyll for a time and may then have served as Abbot of an early foundation at Dryburgh in the borders. Eventually, or so the legends have it, he came north again and founded a church at Falkirk on the site where the Parish Church has stood ever since.

Whatever the origin of the Church it was its arrival which gave rise to the name by which the town and district has been known ever since. But, like the early history of the settlement itself, the evolution of the name during the confused dark age centuries remains a matter for heated debate. From what one scholar called this 'linguistic borderland' came Celtic influences—both the old Welsh or Cumbric and the Irish gaelic—to be overtaken eventually by the middle English of the Anglians. As with so many aspects of the history of this period we must rely on much later written sources. The first reference to the place we know as Falkirk comes in a famous account by one Symeon of Durham written around 1120 but describing events which took place in 1080 not long after the Norman conquest of England:

> In which year the same King William sent his son Robert to Scotland against Malcolm in the autumn. But having turned back when he reached Egglesbreth, he founded New Castle on the river Tyne.

The name 'Egglesbreth' reappears in several later sources following more or less the same form. The 'eggles' part obviously means
church and is associated elsewhere in Scotland with early Christian
foundations, where it is quite often linked with a personal name
giving 'the church of so and so.' In its latin form of 'eccles' one can
think of several examples—Ecclesmachan, the church of St
Machan and Ecclefechan, the church of Fechan. One source does
link two 'welsh' priests or monks with the early church at Falkirk,
a Devyyd and, more interestingly, a Brychan, who appeared to have
been a martyr for the Christian faith. Though the source is some-
what questionable it does fit with a derivation in which the 'breth'
part may then have started life in a cymric form like 'brych' giving
us 'eccles brych' the church of Brych. If this is the case then the
church foundation would predate the Columban mission and be
placed earlier than the 7th century. Which takes us back again to
St Ninian and his followers! What is certain is that when the gaelic
of the Scots from Argyll gradually replaced the earlier celtic form,
Egglesbreth became, not the church of Brych, but Eggles Bhrec,
the broken or speckled church, or Varia Capella as the later latin

A section of Timothy Pont's map of Stirlingshire drawn up around 1590 and
published in Amsterdam in 1654

The so-called foundation stone from the old church of Falkirk which most
observers believe is a 19th century forgery.

manuscripts have it. By turn the gaelic gave way to the language of
the Angles so that by the 12th Century the church, and of course
the settlement nearby are described as Faukirk or Fawkirk—the
speckled or spotted church. One 13th Century document talking
about an earlier period says:

> at length we arrived at Faukirke, which had a nearby cemetery about
> which we inquired, and were then invited into the chapel of the sacred
> house of Mary Magdalene.

Later still the map of the area draw up by the cartographer Timothy
Pont in the late 16th-century and published in Amsterdam in 1654
describes the town as Fakirk. The final touch in the evolution of
the name is amusing particularly to those 'bairns' who still describe
their town as Fa'kirk. Sometime in the 15th Century some pedantic
scribe, thinking no doubt that the Scots ba' really meant ball and
wa' meant wall, decided to turn Fakirk into Falkirk, and thus it has
remained.

The evolution of the name then does suggest an early foundation for the church and, other later evidence talks about the ab or
abbots lands of Falkirk, a term commonly associated with the early
celtic church. Certainly much earlier than the 'foundation stone'
inside the vestibule of the Church which proclaims—'Fundatum
Malcolmo III Rege Scotia AM 1057'. The stone was discovered in
1811 during the rebuilding of the church and was thought by some

to mark the replacement of an early church with a new establishment. Most people now agree that the stone, with its arabic numerals is a forgery, and the finger of suspicion points at the minister of the parish in the early 1800s, Dr James Wilson, who urgently needed such evidence for a lawsuit, and found it in this amazing chance discovery!

In its earliest form the church was probably some kind of monastic settlement with a few missionary monks and an abbot ministering to a small group of people already settled in and around the area of the church. As this form of loose church organisation gradually gave way to the parochial system in the 11th and 12th centuries, Falkirk found itself the centre of a vast parish which stretched all the way from Cumbernauld in the west to the Avon in the east including the later medieval parish of Muiravonside. To the south it reached the boundary of the parish of Slamannan, and to the north the river Carron. By the 12th Century it is recorded as part of the Deanery of Linlithgow within the Bishopric of St. Andrews. The distinguished historian of Falkirk Church, Lewis Lawson confirms Falkirk's relative status at that early period:

> The Deanery of Linlithgow had thirty-five churches, the most richly endowed of which were St Cuthbert's, Edinburgh, cessed at 160 merks, Falkirk cessed at 120 merks and Linlithgow, cessed at 110 merks. The average yield from all thirty five churches was 41 merks so that the importance of Falkirk is evident.

But this apparent prosperity, probably the result of the sheer size of parish as much as on its acknowledged fertility, was not enjoyed in the local area for long, for it was soon being expended on the establishment and maintenance of the Abbey of the Augustian Canons of Holyrood, in Edinburgh. The year 1166 confirmed the gift made by the Bishop of St Andrews:

> Richard, by the grace of God lowly minister of the church of St Andrew to the church of Holyrood and the canons serving God there the church of Eiglesbrec which is called Varia Capella and the whole land which we or any of our ancestors had there with all the pertinents of the said church and lands.

And all this for the annual payment of 'unam petram cerae,' a stone of wax! Thereafter the spiritual needs of local settlement as well as of the scattered souls of the parish fell to these regular priests who enjoyed great popularity with the Kings and nobility of Scotland and whose eighteen houses included Scone, Inchcolm, Cambuskenneth, Inchmahome, and Jedburgh as well as St. Andrews and Holyrood itself. What benefit their skills as farmers and builders brought to Falkirk is unknown—they very probably followed the usual practice of the time by placing a poorly paid vicar with limited education in charge of the parish with the obvious detrimental effects this must have had on what religious life there was among the people. It was to remain like this for four hundred years and scarcely a word has come down to us to illuminate the daily lives of the people as they worked and worshipped, lived and died through war and peace, famine, plague and plenty. We can be sure though, that the church, however badly managed, remained at the heart of the settlement which was, by the time of the great wars of independence, firmly established and now quite definitely called by its English name, Faukirk.

The same darkness which shrouds the early history of Falkirk's church also obscures the origin of the district's second centre of power and influence. Less than a mile to the east stands Callendar House, a huge mansion enclosing behind an imposing Victorian facade, the remains of many centuries, including an early fortified tower house dating from 1400 or thereabouts. But the origins of Callendar go back far beyond this period, and once again, it is the early charters and place name evidence which provides the best, perhaps the only, reliable information.

Several sources in the 11th Century, including an account of William the Conqueror's progress north in 1072, refer to an area called 'Calateria' identified as the huge tract of land between the Rivers Avon and Carron, and including of course, the Falkirk district. We may safely discount a link with the 'Calathros' or 'Calitros' mentioned in accounts of tribal battles of the 7th and 8th Century, but it is a reasonable supposition that before 1000 AD, and probably much earlier, a clearly defined area of vast size in this part of central Scotland emerged, bearing a name recognisable as a version of Callendar. One particularly attractive account found in a French romance of the late 12th Century tells of lady who has a bower in the 'woods of Calitar' where she reposes on a couch covered by a counterpane of a chequered pattern! Maybe woven from a bale of the celebrated Falkirk tartan?

From the 12th Century on, versions of the name appear regularly in royal charters and judgements, which usually link the lands of Callendar with a ruling family enjoying considerable power and wealth. Even at a time when much low lying land was impassable and thousands of acres lay as unusable marsh, moss and scrub, the lands of Callendar included rich woodlands and pasturage, fertile plains, river fishings and saltpans. Confirmation of the power and status of these overlords of Callendar comes with the use of the title 'thane' which appears to have been introduced to Scotland from the south around the 11th Century—Callendar was one of only two areas in Scotland south of the Forth to carry such a distinction.

In 1990 an archaeological dig by Falkirk Museum staff in the area to the east of Callendar House—on the site of the former College—uncovered the foundations of a large wooden building which has been radio-carbon dated to the 9th century. Around 80 feet long by 25 wide, its size and construction is in keeping with the kind of fortification likely to have been required in the turbulent and disordered society which characterised the emerging Scottish nation at that particular period. Interestingly enough the eminence on which the building once stood has been known for many centuries as 'Palace Hill'.

During the reign of King David 1, between 1124 and 1153 the first personal name appears—one Dufoter de Calateria as witness to a charter—and during the same reign we have the first mention of a thane, Duncan by name. During the following sixty years, several others are described as thanes—in 1190 we have 'Malcomo, Theino de Calentar' and in 1226 one 'P'...(probably Patrick), Thane of Callendar', witnessed a Lennox charter. The Lennox connection is an interesting one—as well as the extensive lands between Avon and Carron, the thanes of Callendar also held territory in Kilsyth which was within the lands of the powerful Earls of Lennox. This, coupled with the Callendar Christian names— Malcolm, Duncan and Patrick, all familiar royal Lennox names— has led that sharp-eyed observer, John Reid to suggest that the earliest ruling family of which we have any knowledge may well have been a branch of the Scottish royal family itself.

The last individual described as a thane was another Malcolm who in 1234 gifted lands to the Knights Templar. In the same year, however, it was his lands that were being gifted elsewhere, presumably without his wholehearted support! King Alexander II, conscious perhaps of the growing power of his thanes, or anxious to secure for himself the patronage which huge land holdings would bring, brought the thanage of Callendar to an end. Malcolm was 'bought out' by the crown and received back only a proportion of what his family had once held. The charters covering this change in status make it quite clear who the major beneficiaries of the new arrangements would be:

> Alexander by the grace of God, king of Scots to all men of his whole land, churchmen and laymen, greetings. Let men know, now and to come, that we have given in feu to the canons of the holy cross of Edinburgh for ever all our land in Kalentyr, that we had in hand on the day when we assigned Malcolm, late thane of Kalentyr, forty librates of land.

Thus the same Canons who already owned the small church lands of the 'terrae de Faukirk' in the town itself, and who were entitled to the church revenues from the huge parochial territory, were now also the possessors of the rich lands of what became the Abbot's carse, later Abbots Kerse. The rest of the original territory, still large and valuable, remained a considerable inheritance for thane Malcolm's successors as Knights of Callendar.

Among them we know of one 'Alwin de Kalentyr' in 1252, a 'Sir John de Calentir' around 1296 and later another 'Alwyn,' and finally Patrick in the early 14th century. They were clearly men of substance playing a significant part in the power play of the emerging Scottish nation in the oasis of relative peace and prosperity which proceeded the disastrous wars of independence at the end of the 13th Century. By then their land holding seems to have been further diminished with the emergence of the Stirling family, who found themselves in possession of a large tract of land north of Falkirk later known as West Kerse and held by them and their successors—Monteath, Hope and Dundas—for over six hundred years. The map shows the probable division of land around the end of the 13th Century with Kerse lying north of Falkirk and including a substantial stretch of the Forth, the 'drylands' of Polmont and the summer hill country of the Redding muir. The Stirling's lands

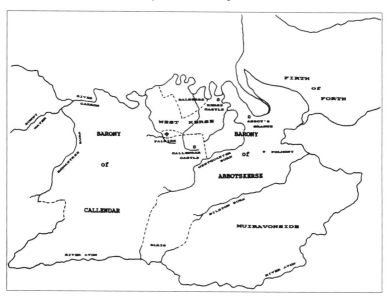

The land divisions in the Falkirk area around 1300 AD showing territory held by
Callendar, Abbotskerse and West Kerse. *Drawing* John Reid.

of West Kerse were smaller but included the area of Bainsford,
Mungall Mill and Middlefield north to the Carron. The rest was
Callendar land with the exception of Dalderse which remained
something of an independent enclave within West Kerse.

When the redoubtable 'Hammer of the Scots' Edward the First
of England crossed into Scotland to punish the effrontery of the
irregular army of Wallace, a large number of the native nobility
including 'Sir John de Calentir' and his son, signed the infamous
Ragman Roll swearing allegiance to the English King. At least one
of these two was in arms against the Scots when the two huge armies
came face to face near Falkirk on 22nd July 1298.

One hundred and eleven noble families with all their retinues
of foot and horse made up a huge force, perhaps thirty thousand
strong which moved westwards from Linlithgow to face a similar
number of Scots in what must have been one of the biggest land
battles ever fought on British soil. Where this mighty clash took
place remains something of a mystery. Over the years antiquaries
and local historians using the few clues available have championed
this or that corner of the Falkirk district, but no agreement has
emerged despite hours of entertaining debate! Tradition, for what

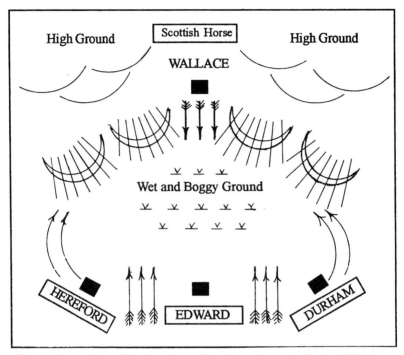

The relative positions of the Scottish and English armies at the Battle of Falkirk
on 22nd July 1298 *Drawing* Ian Scott

it is worth, places the centre of the battle in the area of the present
Victoria Park and street names like Wallace and Campfield remind
us of the connection. We do however know a good deal about the
conduct of the engagement itself which was to prove such a disaster
to Wallace and the Scottish cause. The English knights formed
three columns led by the King himself in the centre, the warlike
Bishop of Durham, Anthony de Beck on the right and the Earls of
Norfolk and Hereford on the left. Separated from them by a stream
or marshy ground, were the Scots, drawn up into three or four
great schiltroms—massive defensive circles or 'phalanx rings' as
they are sometimes called—bristling with twelve foot spears, for all
the world like giant porcupines. Behind them on the high ground
were the mounted nobility, though there were precious few of
them with Wallace and even fewer when they were needed most at
the height of the bloody battle.

The English attacked repeatedly using knights on horseback to

weaken the schiltroms but the Scots held. At this critical stage
Edward called up his archers, whose longbows would later win the
honours at Agincourt and Crecy, but who were now put to the
battle test for the first time. Wallace looked to his horsemen to
scatter them but found that these nobles had left the field. Robert
Bruce may have been one of them, or perhaps he was already in
the ranks of the English King! Whatever, the Scots were doomed.
Great swathes were cut in the rings as wave after wave of arrows
pierced the defence. And now the knights could do their worst on
the open and dispirited Scottish ranks. The rout followed quickly
and Wallace with many of his gallant men fled towards the Carron
and the relative safety of the Torwood. Many hundreds, perhaps
thousands, did not escape and they lie buried today in the common
pits near the field of battle as was the custom. They lie in peace
still for the site has never been found despite seven centuries of
agricultural and industrial development.

The elaborate tomb of Sir John de Graeme and the plain grave slab of Sir John
Stewart in the graveyard of Falkirk Old and St Modans Church.

But the great and powerful among the Scottish fallen were carried to the kirkyard of Falkirk for burial, and there they remain, their graves marked by fine memorials. Sir John de Graeme, Wallace's right-hand according to contemporary accounts, was says the inscription on his tomb, 'ane of the chiefs wha rescewet Scotland thris'. Above him they laid a carved effigy of a knight in armour which has been replaced twice in the intervening years—all three stones remain, caged behind a splendid wrought iron cupola erected by Victorian admirers in 1860. Less grand is the flat stone which marks the grave of Sir John Stewart, whose gallant men of Bute fell to a man in a vain attempt to save their chief. The granite Celtic cross now standing in front of the church near the High Street—the Bute Memorial—was another late salute, this time from the Marquis of Bute in 1877.

Though it is difficult to be sure how many fought or fell at Falkirk on that Magdalen's day, we do have the names of many leading men who were captured and later exchanged for prisoners held by the enemy. Among these was Sir John, Knight of Callendar held by the Scots and freed in exchange for one Reginald le Cheyne, held by the English. Although Sir John and his family continued to support the English crown during the final Scottish triumph at Bannockburn in 1314, they managed to retain their hold on the lands in Falkirk area in the short period of peace which followed. But within a generation they had once again made the wrong choice and were swept aside by a dynasty that would dominate local affairs for four centuries, and ensure that the people of Falkirk were continuously involved in all the great affairs of the nation.

CHAPTER 3

The Livingstons of Callendar

The period of stability which followed the victory at Bannockburn did not survive for long after the death of the Bruce in 1329. In a renewed dispute over the rightful succession, a Bailiol challenger took up arms once again supported by the English and by a section of the Scottish nobility including, predictably enough, the Callendars. The defeat of King David II at Neville's Cross and his imprisonment at Durham no doubt brought brief advantage to the then incumbent 'Patrick de Calentyre' but vengeance soon followed the King's release and restoration. In 1346 all the lands of Patrick were forfeit and given instead to one William Livingston, whose loyalty had brought him to the same English prison as the King. The Livingstons were a family holding lands in West Lothian, but now they moved to the centre of the Scottish stage and for four centuries were seldom far from the fulcrum of power. But that was in the future. In a time of rapidly changing fortunes, William's principal concern was to secure the new possessions for his family, and he did so by the traditional method. Marriage to Christiane de Calentyre daughter of the deposed Patrick, went a long way to protect the claim of their descendants against whatever the unpredictable winds of political change might bring in the future.

From this substantial base, the Livingstons grew in power and influence. Sir William's son John fell fighting alongside King Robert III at Homildon Hill in 1402 and when King James I was murdered in 1436 it was Sir Alexander Livingston, the next Knight of Callendar who spirited away the six year old James II and later became the King's Guardian, Justiciary of Scotland, and effective Regent during the King's minority. But power in those turbulent times depended ultimately on an individual noble's willingness to take up arms against others who challenged their position and, on more than one occasion, Sir Alexander and his Falkirk vassals burned and demolished the strongholds of their enemies. He even had the audacity to besiege his erstwhile ally Crichton in the castle of Edinburgh, the very place where the two had brutally murdered a Douglas rival following the notorious 'black dinner' of 1439. But such actions provoke equally ferocious reactions and the Knight of Callendar was often forced to defend his lands and castle from vengeful and ambitious rivals. About 1444 we hear of a young Douglas nobleman attacking Livingston lands in Falkirk and destroying the castle of Callendar, followed by a predictably powerful reply from Sir Alexander and his allies. And, underlining the rapid ebb and flow of fortune, we find just a few years later, both Alexander and his son confined in the Castle of Dumbarton as the King's enemies. Within months they were not only free but again enjoying positions of power at the same King's right hand. Confused and confusing times indeed! But these were the conditions which a succession of child monarchs brought to Scotland during the next century and a half, and there was always a Livingston close to the centre of affairs, most often playing a full part in the intrigue and double dealing which so scarred this particular page of Scotland's story.

Sir Alexander's son Sir James, was also the King's Guardian and became the Great Chamberlain of Master of the Royal Household. He was rewarded with a Lordship of Parliament by the King and the title first Lord Livingston of Callendar. After James II's death in 1460 he remained as 'magnus camerarius' during the minority of the new King and served as ambassador to the English court. In his later years he was once again involved in intrigue to secure greater control over the young James 111 and for a period the family's influence at court declined, though they continued to enjoy complete power in the Barony of Callender which was confirmed in 1458.

The original thane's house was probably replaced in the early fifteenth century by a strongly fortified tower house, elements of which remain within the western end of the present Callendar House. The church at Falkirk was completely rebuilt in the 1450s and included a south aisle to house the dead of the new Livingston dynasty, an important step in the growth of power and status. About this time one brother 'Henricus de Levingstoun' is recorded as Knight Commander of the Order of St John of Jerusalem in Scotland and Preceptor of Torphichen. The order acquired some rights in the south aisle of the church which was converted into a chapel for their order dedicated to St John as well as the last resting place of the feudal lords of Callendar.

The pre Reformation church of Falkirk and the roof boss showing the Livingston coat of arms from around 1450.

The new church building followed the traditional catholic west-east alignment with a second aisle to the north dedicated to St. Michael the Archangel. The western nave, eastern chancel and the two aisles were joined together by a great square tower with 'lofty arches' housing the altar. This square tower survived the rebuilding of 1811 and remains as the vestibule of the present building, though the arches lie buried behind the brick and plaster of a new age. At the crossing point of the church above the altar was a great stone roof boss bearing the arms of Livingston of Callendar and this has survived and can be seen in the west corridor of the present church. So too have the effigies of two of the feudal lords and their ladies, but they are so badly weathered as to make identification difficulty though early scholars thought

The Livingston effigies from Falkirk Old and St Modans Parish Church -
probably those of Lord William Livingston and his wife from around 1590. The
drawing was done by Fleming in 1902.

one pair may represent the King's guardian Sir Alexander or his
son. The second pair date from the next century.

It was with another Alexander, the fifth Lord that the Livingstons
returned to the centre of the political stage, for he was close to
King James V and accompanied him to France in 1537 to celebrate
his brief marriage to the Princess Magdalene. When the King died
in 1542—a broken man whose armies had been roundly defeated
by the English at Solway Moss—the care of his infant daughter,
Mary, then a few days old, was entrusted to eight nobles, one of
whom was Sir Alexander Livingston. It was the beginning of a close
personal relationship between the ill-fated Queen and the Livingston family which ended forty-five years later on the scaffold of
Fotheringay Castle in 1587.

King Henry VIII of England, like his predecessors before him, feared the constant threat from his northern neighbour and hoped now to win the Scottish crown for his infant son Edward by arranging a marriage between him and the Queen of Scots. The Earl of Arran, acting as Regent of Scotland favoured such an arrangement but a powerful group led by the Earl of Moray and Cardinal Beaton and including Lord Alexander Livingston were bitterly opposed. On 4th September 1543 at Callendar House the parties were reconciled and joined in a rejection of Henry's proposal. From then on Livingston along with Lord Erskine was entrusted with the care of the young Queen lest she fall into the hands of the enemy. Thus the Privy Council Register of 5th June 1546 records:

> the Lordis Erskine and Levingstown Lordis chosin to be of Secret Counsel, ... of the keeping of our Soverane Ladis persoun.

Henry was far from happy with the outcome and his armies invaded Scotland seeking revenge for the insult given. At Pinkie on 10 September 1547 hundreds of Scots fell in battle, among them Lord Livingston's son and heir John, Master of Livingston who had led a party of vassals from Falkirk in his father's name. The threat to the Queen was increased and in August 1548 she sailed to France to begin a twelve year period away from her homeland.

As companions Mary had with her four daughters of noble families—Mary Fleming, Mary Seton, Mary Beaton and Mary Livingston of Callendar. These four Maries were about the same age as the Queen and were to remain with her for much of her troubled life. The ballad writers, never over concerned about accuracy, have served the Livingston memory badly for only Seton and Beaton made it into the famous song. Who the 'Mary Carmichael' or the Mary Hamilton of the song's title were, no one is certain. Lord Alexander accompanied his daughter and the young Queen to France and died there some five years later. His part in this most famous story is comemorated by a badly worn grave slab from the old Livingston aisle which bears an incomplete inscription as follows:

> ALE(xander) ADOLESCENTIAM PROVECTAM AE TATEMINVLA REGUM GALLIAE ....

which seems to confirm his role as the protector of the young Queen in France. The slab also bears the Livingston coat of arms along with the device of his wife Lady Agnes Douglas. On his death the title Lord of Callendar passed to his son Lord William Livingston who remained in Scotland and was to play a significant part in bringing Mary Queen of Scots back to her Kingdom in 1561.

It was during the Queen's sojourn in France that the stirring events of the Reformation transformed the religious and political face of Scotland, though Falkirk seems to have escaped the attention of the more extreme among the reformers. Indeed it appears that the last Catholic vicar, a man named Hogge, demitted office quietly and his congregation, if he still had one, adopted the new theology without fuss. The new Lord of Callendar was an enthusiastic supporter of the change, but his new found Protestantism did not diminish one whit his devotion to the young Catholic Queen. Indeed he was one of a group of nobles who journeyed to France in 1560 to invite Mary to return to Scotland, which she did the following August.

There followed the best known and most often recounted period in the life of the Queen—seven tumultuous years in which she married twice, gave birth to a son and heir, suffered imprisonment, braved defeat on the battlefield and fled to what was to be a long English exile ended only by her execution in 1587. Throughout this period the Livingstons of Callendar were among her closest personal friends and allies. Lord William's wife Agnes was the Queen's cousin and sister of Mary Fleming, one of the four Maries, and from the Queen's arrival in Scotland in 1561 it was clear that Callendar House would be a regular port of call. In 1565 she was present at the magnificently celebrated marriage of Mary Livingston—one of her 'maries'—to John, son of Lord Robert Sempill and, from her the couple were gifted Crown lands, including Auchtermuchty and the island of Little Cumbrae, a wedding dress for the bride and a number of other presents including 'ane bed of scarlet velvot bordered with broderie of blak velvot'. John Knox, ever ready to damn those close to the Queen, wrote in his History that 'It was weill knawin that schame haistit mariage betwix John Semphill, callit the Danser, and Marie Levingstoune, surnameit the Lustie'. Not for the first time the evidence does not support this particular slur.

A few months after the Livingston wedding, on 1st July 1565, the

Queen was in Callendar House for the baptism of one of Lord Livingston's children which followed the protestant form which Mary found abhorrent. Nonetheless she stayed to hear the sermon preached, we are told, by Knox himself, because, as she told her host, she wished 'to show him (Lord William) that favour that she had not done to any other before'. She remained in Falkirk for several days on this occasion though already her enemies, incensed by her engagement to Henry, Lord Darnley, were on the roads seeking to waylay her and her noble supporters. Three weeks later she married Darnley and began the downward acceleration of her fortunes which ended with her exile.

On the 9th March 1566 Livingston was one of the Lords in attendance on the Queen at Holyrood House when her Italian secretary and confidante David Riccio was brutally murdered by associates of Darnley; indeed there is some suggestion that his own life was threatened and with Huntly, Bothwell, Fleming and others he was forced to flee from the Palace to a place of refuge. Three months later as the Queen prepared to give birth to the future James VI in Edinburgh Castle, Mary Livingston helped her draw up a list of her possessions which has survived in "Les Inventaires de la Royne Descosse". It includes numerous references to the Livingston family with details of gifts to the dowager Lady Living-ston and her two daughters Mary and Magdalen, who was herself one of the Queen's maids of honour after her sister's marriage, and who is always referred to as 'Livingston la jeusne'- the younger. On the occasion already mentioned Magdelen was to have re-ceived: 'Une aultre montre garny de dourze rubiz et deux grandes saffiz avec une perle pandant au bout'. When the same lady married Arthur Erskine of Blackgrange, himself a favourite royal equery, she was presented with among other things: 'Une vasquine de toille d'or cramosysye brodee d'une petitte frange d'or'.

During the month of January 1567, Mary stayed three separate nights at Callendar House—the 13th when passing from Stirling to Edinburgh with her infant son, the 24th when en route to visit the smallpox ridden Darnley in Glasgow, and the 27th when both she and her husband rested for a night during their return journey to Edinburgh. Two weeks later Darnley was murdered in the Kirk o' Field and James Hepburn, Earl of Bothwell, thought by many to have organised the crime, began to play a major part in the Queen's final six months of power. On 24th April he carried her

The embroidered panel from Callendar House with the MS monogram.

off to Dunbar Castle and she agreed to marry him. On 15th May at four in the morning in Holyrood, the marriage was celebrated following protestant forms and Lord Livingston was one of only eight noblemen present. The Lords who opposed the marriage and the Queen, took to arms and at Carberry Hill they defeated her adherents. Mary we are told was hurried on foot through the streets of Edinburgh in her nightgown supported by her faithful companions Mary Livingston and Mary Seton. She was sent to Lochleven Castle.

On 29th June in Dumbarton, Lord Livingston and other loyal nobles denounced the Queen's imprisonment and called on all loyal people to take up arms on her behalf. Support was slight and the Queen was forced to abdicate the throne in favour of her infant son. The Earl of Moray became Regent and on the 10th September he met a deputation of Mary's adherents, including Lord Livingston, to discuss her release. Again they were unsuccessful in their appeals and she remained confined until her escape in May the following year. Livingston supported by men from Falkirk fought beside her at Langside and he was with her as she left the country for exile in England. Lady Livingston joined them shortly afterwards.

Of course the Callendar House known to Mary Queen of Scots and witness to many of these great events was quite different from the building we know today. But behind the Victorian facade at the west end lies the plain oblong 'castle' not much bigger that the square tower with which the house originally began life. For many years from the mid Victorian era, the apartments said to have been used by Mary were devoted to displays of paintings and engravings depicting her life and times but these were disposed of by auction in 1961. One fascinating item among the collection was a beautiful example of embroidery with the monogram M.S. in the centre. It has recently been dated to the mid-16th Century and the style and workmanship suggest that it may be from the hand of one of the Maries or even the Queen herself—she was certainly known to be a very accomplished needlewoman and did make gifts of her work to her favourites. Whatever the truth, it remains as a tangible reminder of the link between the House and its most famous visitor.

The devotion of the Livingstons did not end with the departure of the Queen to confinement in a succession of English castles and great houses. Both Sir William and his wife spent much of the next twenty years either by her side or on missions, both official and secret, aimed at securing her release and return to power. In 1569 an English agent visiting Tutbury Castle reported:

> The greatest personadge in house abowte hir is the Lord of Levenston and the lady his wife, which is a fayre gentilwoman; and it was told me both Protestants.

Around 1572 while her husband was in France on business for the Queen, Lady Livingston returned to Falkirk where she was allowed to use her home on condition that it should not be used as a refuge for 'rebels or declared traitors'. Despite this undertaking the secret work continued and the Lady soon found herself confined in Dalkeith Castle where we are told that:

> although things were so evident that she could not deny them, she would confess nothing except by tears and silence.

The struggle for power in Scotland continued throughout the Queen's long imprisonment, centred as ever on the possession of the young monarch. Successive Regents faced constant challenges from other powerful rivals as well as from the supporters of the Queen. And it was such rivalry that almost brought Falkirk yet another battle to add to the long list of engagements fought in and around this particular stretch of central Scotland.

In 1578 the King, aged twelve, was in Stirling Castle under the control of the Regent James Douglas, Earl of Morton. The so called Marian Lords, especially Atholl and Argyll supported as ever by the Livingston loyalists from Falkirk marched with an army of close on four thousand men towards the town bearing a blue 'sarsnet',that is, silk, banner showing the young King looking through a barred window with the words 'Liberty I crave and cannot have it' and, more menacingly, 'Either you shall have it or we will die for it'. The army, forever after known to their enemies as the 'faction of the Falkirk', came face to face with Morton advancing from Stirling to meet them with a force of equal strength and determination. Another bloody clash seemed inevitable. Archbishop Spotiswoode of Glasgow was an eyewitness:

> When they were on the point of engaging, the men handling their arms, and the chiefs riding from post to post conveying their orders, a trumpet sounded; and, when its echo had died away,there was a pause of a moment, then at another flourish of bugles, Sir Robert Bowes, the English ambassador, rode up attended by his suite, and stationed himself between the hostile ranks. He rode from chief to chief, entreating them to forbear from fighting; and at length, by proposing honourable terms, he succeeded in persuading them to agree to a truce

But before the treaty was concluded a personal challenge was made, and accepted:

> A cavalier, of the name of Tait, a follower of the Laird of Cessford, who

was at Falkirk in arms against Morton, cased in complete steel, rode
out between the lines,bearing his glove on the point of his lance, and
having thrown it before the enemies ranks, challenged any one of them
to break a lance for his mistress. The pledge was lifted by a soldier of
the name of Johnston, who was an attendant on the master of Glamis,
and the challenge accepted. A place was immediately marked out for
the combat; it was a little level plain on the banks of the Carron, on
both sides of which river the horsemen stood spectators. It was about
sunset on a calm autumn evening, 1578, when the combatants entered
the lists; they sat on horseback, and remained at opposite extremitie
of the course, till the signal was given, when they couched their spears,
and rode at full gallop against each other. At the first shock, Tait was
transfixed by his antagonist's lance; his hands lost hold of his arms and
his bridle; he drooped his head, tumbled from his saddle, and died.

While these great national events were engaging the energies of
the Lords of Callander and their families, what was happening
to the village or town of Falkirk itself? Only part of the present
town centre—roughly north, and due east of the church, was
within the lands of Abbot's Kerse—the remainder to the south
including the present High Street was Callendar territory. The
parish church was of course the common link between these two
centres of power and it seems likely that the early village grew
up, around and away from, the church along two roads—one
along modern Manor Street and Kerse Lane, down Ladysmill
towards the lands of Kerse and the other leading to the 'castle'
of Callendar possibly following Manor Street, Silver Row and
East Bridge Street and across the East Burn to Callendar. By the
mid-15th century when the church was rebuilt the small population, perhaps three or four hundred, probably lived in an
assortment of stone and wooden buildings in closes and wynds off
these narrow thoroughfares. By 1500 some of the land in the area
immediately north-west of the church in modern Newmarket
Street, as well as the land at the east end of the 'King's High Road'
was being feued by both Holyrood and Callendar. The beginning
of the expansion of the town might be dated from then for some
reports in the early 1800s talk of old stone buildings on the High
Street bearing the date 1513. In addition, certain old legal titles to
buildings on the south side of the High Street suggest that they
were built on feus from the 'hospital at Torphichen' which

possessed glebe lands connected with the south aisle of the church at that period.

Fifty years later the Reformation brought the former church lands into the hands of a lay commendator who had the right to draw revenues formerly destined for the canons of Holyrood. Attempts to take advantage of this reorganisation led to tension between these new masters and the Callendar faction in the divided town, and as early as 1566 followers of the two clashed and blood was spilled. There followed an injunction from the Privy Council against such behaviour, to be read at the mercat crosses in Stirling and Falkirk. This is the earliest record of such a cross in Falkirk which at that time did not enjoy the status signified by a mercat cross, nor the power to arrange markets, control trade, license merchants and manufacturers and levy charges which flowed from it. It may be that the commendator had decided to transfer some of the rights of the Barony of Kerse to the town as a way of increasing revenue and that this met with resistance from the jealous Callendar men. In the 1580s control of Kerse passed to a new commendator, Sir John Bellenden, Laird of Broughton near Edinburgh, and for a period from 1587 on the town was officially part of the Barony of Broughton! In the same year there is a record of men trading in Falkirk though the nature and extent of this is unknown.

It is about this period that the five town gates or ports were built. Their location is uncertain though it seems likely that one stood on the present High Street near the Lint Riggs, another, Westquarter Port, at the entry to the modern Howgate Centre, one in Kirk Wynd near the Bank Street opening, and the fourth on the Cow Wynd. The last one, the east port, probably stood near the point where Silver Row met the High Street. Although not a trace of these now remain, and no archaeological dig has pinpointed their position, one or two of them survived long enough to have been seen and described by antiquaries in the early 1800s:

The ports were built in 1585; they were arched gateways of stone, battlemented at top, with arrow or hagbut loopholes in the side walls. It is not long since the East Port was taken down, and one time-blackened arch is still remaining opposite 'the Lodging Yard' The date, 1585, is discernable on a stone which was taken from the West Port when it was demolished, thirty or forty years ago. This port long hung over the street in a half ruined state, and there was a circular, sloping vizzying hole, through which the armed porter might reconnoitre those who demanded entrance.

Formidable as they sound, there is no evidence that these gates formed part of a full-walled defensive system—indeed later information suggests a series of low stone walls joining buildings or the back ends of properties together as a territorial marker and defence against wandering sheep rather than invading enemies!

By end of the 16th Century, Livingston family support for the Stewarts brought the seventh Lord of Callendar, Alexander to prominence as part of the King's party. Even before he succeeded his father he was a close confidante of the royal favourite Esme Stuart, Duke of Lennox and acted as a trusted messenger between the two when the catholic Duke was exiled at the behest of the Scottish parliament. On one occasion in the 1580s he marched with a troop of men from Falkirk and captured the town and castle of Stirling from the King's enemies and in 1600 he was once again on hand with his men to help rescue King James during the notorious Gowrie conspiracy. A few years earlier, the young Princess Elizabeth, who in later life would marry Frederick, the Elector Palatine and thus give rise to the Hanovarian succession to the British throne, was given into the care of the Livingstons and spent much of her early years at Callendar House. The Scottish churchmen were outraged at this for Lady Livingston was 'an obstinat an profest Papist', but the King had his way. A second royal princess Margaret who died in infancy, was also placed with Lord Alexander in confirmation of King James' determination to resist such pressure.

Two very important rewards flowed from this service and the years of loyal support which preceded it. At the end of 1600 Lord Alexander was created first Earl of Linlithgow and, earlier the same year, the King raised Falkirk, or the Callendar part of it, to the status of a free burgh of barony

> granting to its inhabitants power of buying or selling and of creating burgesses, of having a market cross and holding weekly markets on Thursdays and two fair days a year on 29 June and 26 October; with power to the said Alexander to approve guards of the said fairs and market days and with the power of choosing bailies and of building a

court house....and moreover he erects the whole into a free regality with the power to hold justice courts.

................and all of this in return for 'one pair of gilt spurs to be rendered at the castle of Callendar every year at Whitsunday'. It is in many ways the birth certificate of the burgh of Falkirk—while it did not at that stage apply to the whole town, it laid the basis for all the developments which followed. Any conflict between the baronies which might have arisen was avoided because by 1600 moves to unite the two were well underway. The marriage in 1587 between the then Baron Broughton and Margaret Livingston, sister of Sir Alexander produced a son, Sir James Bellenden who, in 1606 conveyed the lands of Kerse including his part of Falkirk, to his uncle Sir Alexander Livingston. For the first time since the 13th Century, the whole of the town lay under one jurisdiction.

CHAPTER 4

Kirk Session and Baron Court

It was in the early years of the 17th Century during Alexander's time that the first surviving account of life in the town was begun—the sessional records of Falkirk Parish Church, which detail the regular meetings of the minister and elders from 1617 on. These carefully maintained and preserved records provide an invaluable insight into the day to day life of the community albeit filtered through the eyes of the stern elders as they dealt with countless 'scandalous persones for their reformatione'. Much has been written elsewhere about this uniquely Scottish institution with its seemingly insatiable appetite for the gossip and general tittle-tattle which formed a substantial part of the agenda for their fornightly meetings in hundreds of parishes throughout the land. Falkirk was certainly no different from all the others and in charity we should say that the motivation of many, perhaps the majority, was a genuine belief that by calling sinners to an honest repentance they were doing them the best possible service. They were certainly following the guidance given them by the founding fathers who had decreed that

> it stands in reproving and correcting of those faults which the civil sword doth either neglect, either may not punish—drunkenness, excess, be it in apparel or be it in eating and drinking, fornication, oppression of the poor by exactions, deceiving of them in buying and selling by wrong mete or measure, wanton words, or licentious living.

Thus the elders of Falkirk had plenty of scope to search and pry and they used it to the maximum. The swearers and fornicators, drinkers and idlers, the sabbath breakers and disturbers of the peace found themselves regularly summonsed to 'compear' before the Session to answer for their particular brand of scandal. Most came when called, and subjected themselves to interrogation and remonstrance as well as the usual public repentance, normally 'three several sabbaths' at the pillar or stool of repentence plus a public dressing down from the Minister during the service.

Desecrating the sabbath by doing anything at all except praying brought many an early Falkirk 'bairn' to the notice of the elders. In an agricultural area where nature was no respecter of the laws of church or state, many people worked as the need arose and it comes as no great surprise to find 'stacking of corne', 'shearing', 'picking pease' 'carting divots', 'driving cattle' and 'yoking a pleuch' among the regular charges. Many other Sunday diversions also attracted the attention of the all-seeing session and those who were found 'meeting and talking in the street after publick worship' or 'drinking wi' Hielandmen' or 'fighting in the open fields' or even 'idly gazing from windows', could expect little mercy! Pity the poor soul who was called up to answer the claim that he had been seen 'walking fast on the Sabbath', presumably guilty by implication, in that if you walk fast you are obviously on your way to do something, and that, whatever it might be, was not allowed on Sunday!

Excessive drinking was an early besetting sin of Falkirk people and one which lasted well into modern times. The Kirk's vain attempts to stamp it out, and to eliminate the 'horrid swearing' which usually went with it, are confirmed by regular entries in the records of this early period. Even the church officer was not exempt though he seems to have been allowed to break almost every ordinance in the book before he was finally removed from office— a rare flash of charity in such unforgiving times:

16th June 1625

The Session having taken into consideration the prophane and wicked life of John Dun, occasionit by his druckinnes and evile dispossitioun, and notwithstanding of monie grose and oppin faultis qlk hes bein comittit be him in tyme past to the hie offence of God and evile exampill to uyris......of his leudness, filthie druckinnes and wicked lyfe....and shameles behaviour under cloude of nicht.

Then there were those who fought in church over a seat, women who nagged their husbands, pipers and fiddlers who played at weddings and christenings against the orders of the session, and even those rash enough to slander their 'betters' like the Falkirk tailor in 1624 who was ordered;

> for his misbehaviour and unbreading speiches to Dame Margaret Crawford, Lady Dorrator, to go doune on his kneis and ask hir forgiveness publicklie in the kirk.

One other musician who fell foul of the session from time to time was the town drummer, George Brocklay, a cooper whose task was to call the people together for a special announcement at the mercat cross or to lead criminals through the town before their banishment 'furth the paroch of Falkirk'. George was called up before the session accused of:

> drinking and tonkering ye drum at unseasonable hours on ye sabbath morne.

Most often the church punished wrong doers in its own way but occasionally the civil authorities were called in where some form of corporal punishment was thought appropriate. This usually took the form of a threat rather than an actual sentence, though we may be sure that the drunken cooper was called on many a time to signal the public whipping and eviction of undesirables:

28th May 1635

> Nicolas Anderson enacted herself to undergo banishment, and never to be seen in this boundis againe, otherwise to be scourget through the toune of Falkirk or drowned as salbe thoucht most convenient.

Convenient to the session or baillies and not poor Nicolas presumably! But reform of the Scottish church gave Falkirk people much more than a new range of sanctions on their behaviour. The early years of the 17th century saw the beginnings, albeit haltingly at first, of a system of basic schooling and of poor relief. John Knox and his colleagues had called for a school in every parish charged with the task of equipping the 'priesthood of all believers' to read the scripture that would speak directly to them. As a side benefit improved education would assist the development of the community's trade and manufactures.

In 1594 Thomas Ambrose, the first Falkirk 'dominie' of whom we have any information, was deposed for unacceptable behaviour, probably immorality, but soon after he was restored after special pleading from the parishioners. Early in the new century, there is mention of one James Johnstoun, a 'reader' whose 'lyff hes bein good and without scandal' but was not properly qualified to teach. Under pressure from the local Presbytery the Falkirk minister

> promises to use diligence to get ane qualified master iff they will find him sufficient maintenance. The brethren thinks it meit that the Erle of Linlithgow, the patrone, be requested that he would give his assistance for the furtherance of so good a work as to have ane schoole their for instructioun and educasun of youth.

By 1632, this seems to have been achieved because the master, John Dishingtoun, who was also Session Clerk and precentor of the psalms, was earning £40 Scots. Thereafter the school appears to have become an established part of parochial activity though where the children met and what they studied beyond reading is not known. In 1644 the Session underlined their determination to extend the provision:

> all the children within the town who had past sex years of age should be put to the comon schole kept for the present be Mr James Levingstoun and if there wer any whose parents wer not able to pay for them, in that case he should teach them gratis.

Despite the best efforts of the elders there is evidence that others were offering education for fees and that such adventure or dame schools were drawing children away from the parochial school. In 1656 for example, the Session banned women from 'keeping any school', but later, relented so far as to allow a woman to teach sewing and weaving to girls but on no account 'the reiding'. Later still one Grizel Kincaid was forbidden to 'meddle with the teaching of male children'. John Forest, James Nicol, William Drummond and Patrick Renny followed one another as parochial teachers apparently using a succession of unsatisfactory rented houses and constantly fighting to secure the legal salary for the job. It was a situation that would continue almost unchanged for the next two centuries.

The relief of the poverty had always been a church responsibility which the Kirk Sessions of the new reformed church determined to continue and develop. Regular collection and distribution of funds to relieve the hardship of the deserving poor became a regular feature of Scottish church life with those on the approved parish list being paid a small amount each month. Vagabonds from other areas were denied any support and even begging was licensed, and limited to official parochial beggers!

But in common with kirk sessions in every part of Scotland, the majority of the Falkirk elders time was taken up with up identifying and punishing what the early fathers called, with commendable bluntness 'fornication'. Later on, the clerks would search for softer expressions like 'uncleanness' or even 'social impurity,' but the meaning was the same, and any young Falkirk couple who made the mistake of holding hands, might find themselves on the long list of offenders grilled by the elders at every meeting. Three Sundays of public humiliation usually followed but if adultery, a much more heinous crime, was involved then a more severe punishment was meted out. The earliest record of such a case in Falkirk occurred on 7th January, 1619 when the couple involved were ordered to pay a fine of five pounds and,

> stand at the kirk dore, bare futtit and bair legit for several Sabathis, from the first bell to the last, and thereafter to pass to the stool of repentence in sec claithis everie day of the said sex Sabathis in tyme of sermone.

With services lasting three hours in a dark and damp kirk with no heating and a bare earthen floor, such punishment in a Scottish winter must have been almost impossible to bear, yet the evidence suggests that, for the most part, the people accepted the iron rule and were prepared for almost any punishment rather than lose the 'sealing ordinances' of baptism and communion for themselves or their children. Indeed there are even incidents where enthusiasm for the service was itself a cause for disapproval, as when one man was accused of

> misbehaviour and trublance of the Kirk upone Pasche Day, by lowping in at the windo after the dores were clossit and the sermoun began.

James Livingston of Almond, first Earl of Callendar and his coat-of-arms.

The elders accepted his claim that 'it was for the earnest he had to heir the Word preachit and to communicat of the Sacrament'. Such communion services were held only once or twice each year and they were very big affairs drawing hundreds of visitors to the town from other parishes over a period of three or four days before the 'occasion' itself. The people's determination not to miss out on the big day is confirmed by one of the earliest visitors to the area in 1643. Gilbert Blakhal, described interestingly enough as 'priest of the Scots mission in France, in the low countries and in Scotland', arrived in Bo'ness late at night:

> I went to sie my horse suppe and then called for my bedde, as if I had been wearyed, and paying myn hostesse at night was mounted upone my hors by the brack of day, and passing by the Falkirk, a place where Walas resorted oft, I did see the country people whigging their meres to be tymously at the kirk, as if they had been running for a pryse. They passed me, bidding me spurre my hors to communicat with them, to whom I gave no answer, but did ride softly to the end of the Torrewoode when I did find an ailehouse all alone.

If Gilbert was in Scotland to assess the prospects for a revival of Catholic fortunes he picked a bad time for by then the country was embroiled in a dispute which would take the church even further from the old style of liturgy and church government. Once again the Livingstons of Callendar were in the thick of the argument.

When Charles 1 succeeded his father to the united thrones of Scotland and England in 1625 it was clear from the outset that his personal adherence to episcopalian forms would eventually lead him into conflict with his presbyterian countrymen north of the border. In the event more than a decade passed before the affair reached a crisis when an attempt by Charles to force the Scots into submission provoked armed resistance in the so called Bishops Wars. For the first time in almost three centuries a Livingston took up arms against a Stewart King. This was James, Lord Almond, who in 1633 had purchased the lands of Callendar from his elder brother Alexander, the eighth Lord Livingston. A staunch presbyterian and a very experienced soldier, he signed the National Covenant in 1638, promising to defend the liberty of the Scottish church against the King's encroachments. But like his great contemporary Montrose, he was both covenanter and royalist, and for a decade he would agonise over every decision which threatened to place the two on opposite sides. In 1640 he joined Montrose and several other nobles in the Cumbernauld Bond, a secret agreement to defend both King and covenant against what they saw as the evil intent of Argyll and the Scottish church party. Despite this he accepted, albeit reluctantly, the post of second-in-command to General Alexander Leslie in the powerful Scottish army which marched into England later the same year. In the face of such resistance the King soon gave way and a peace agreement followed. In the aftermath the King rewarded the leaders of the Scots— Argyll, Leslie, and Almond who was created first Earl of Callendar. In the same year, 1641, he was offered the post of Treasurer to the King, but the Scottish estates, aware now of the Cumbernauld Bond, refused to sanction the appointment.

Despite this easing of the situation the King's determination to have the Scots submit to his religious view kept the new Earl on the side of the Kirk, and when the civil war in England broke out in 1642 James Livingston was once again among the commanders of the Scots army against the King. The Falkirk Session made its position clear when the new Solemn League and Covenant was signed in the church, with great care taken to ensure that all took part:

> October 31st, 1643 It is ordained that on Sunday when the Covenant shall be subscribed, the persons following shall attend the several parts if the kirk, viz: To attend the north isle, Wastquarter and Patrick Grindlay; to attend the wast end of the kirk, John Monteath and John Wyse; to attend the east end, Walter Scott and Patrick Guidlat; to attend the wast loft, Alexander Watt and Hew Hall; to attend the east loft, Robert Burn and Patrick Guidlat.

Thus blessed by the local fathers and brethern, James and his Falkirk vassals marched off once again to war, fighting on the side of the Parliament against the King at Marston Moor and at Carlisle. When Charles surrendered to the Scots, Callendar was one of the leaders who spend long hours with the King trying to persuade him to relax his religious demands and reconcile himself with his natural supporters in Scotland. Though unsuccessful in this, Callendar's attachment to the royal cause seems to have led to a personal understanding with the King for in 1646 the town of

Falkirk was once again elevated in status. The baronies of Kerse and Callendar were united into a single free regality with Falkirk as its head burgh. New powers were conferred on James in relation to the control of trade and manufacture and the administration of justice within the town, and for the first time it was in a position to match in prestige and power, the rival royal burghs of Linlithgow and Stirling.

Within twelve months the Earl, disturbed by the way in which the victorious Parliamentarians were acting in both religious and political affairs, led his battle weary men from Falkirk to war for the last time in a desperate attempt to save the King. This great 'engagement', as it was called, was frowned upon by the Scottish Kirk, including the elders of Falkirk, and the Earl and his men were later condemned by the Kirk Session which wished no truck with episcopal Stewart Kings. In the event it was a disaster as Cromwell's new model army swept the Scots aside with ease. Near Preston in August 1648 the Scots were crushed and Callendar with his Falkirk cavalry broke out from the closing circle of the enemy and eventually escaped to the north and home to the hostile arms of the kirk. James Livingston himself made his way in disguise to London and escaped to Holland where he joined the party surrounding the exiled Prince Charles.

Over the next few years the Session dealt with seventy-five Falkirk soldiers along with officers like 'Sir William Levingstone of Wastquarter, lieutenant-colonel and governor of the toune of Carlyl', 'Sir Alexander Levingstoune, ane leavetennant-colonal to ane regiment of hors' and, 'Sir William Callander of Dorrator, captain-leavetennant to ane hors troup'. All declared themselves 'sorriful and willing to obey ye kirk'.

Throughout these stormy events and beyond through the century, the people of the town carried on with their everyday business seemingly undisturbed by the power struggles waged in their name far from home. It is a period rich in source material for apart from the sessional records, we also have the detailed reports of the Court Book of Callendar from 1638 to around 1715, in which the baillies of Falkirk dispense justice in the name of 'ane nobill and potent Lord James Lord Levingstowne of Almont and Callender'. It is an amazing document full of fascinating details which illuminate the lives of the ordinary working people of the district. Here are the indwellers of the town, the 'portioners, feweris and tennentis' along with the tradesmen—'smithes, and wrights, fleschors, websters and baxteris, maltmen, cordiners and tailyers' and, of course, the powerful 'mairtchands'—settling disputes, pursuing claims and receiving judgements on matters of slight or great importance by turns. But this was no mighty lord laying down the law to cringing vassals, but baillies who are themselves portioners and merchants, farmers and maltmen resolving disputes among their peers so that a well regulated trading environment is available for all—or at least all those who bore the official seal of approval:

4th December 1638

Item ... that na induellar within the said toune of Falkirk use any traffique or mak any mairthandice within the said burgh thairof except onlie those quha is admittit burgesss of the said burgh and hes ressavit from his lordschip burgess tyckettis and quhasoevar doethe in the contrair heirof to pey X li

There many examples of the Court trying to protect community assets:

7th January 1642

The quhilk day it is statute and ordanit That the haill scheipe be put furthe of the towne of Falkirk befoir any peis be sawne under the paine of 40ss and that na bairnes cum within the said peis in tyme of hervest....and that fowles be keipit in housss fra the first of mairtche untill the first of June.

And there are judgements on the ownership of a horse—or a house, on money borrowed and not repaid, on goods ordered but not supplied, and cloth supplied but not paid for. Most often the punishments are financial penalties, in part to right the wrong but in part no doubt to swell the coffers of 'ane potent and nobil lord'!

When the people stepped out of line to resolve their differences in a more direct way, the Court was always ready to make them pay for the pleasure:

5th Appryle 1639

And anent the complaint gevine in befoir the said bailzies be Hendrie
Hall in Falkirk againis Patrick Muirhead maltman thair ffor casting of
ane glasful of beir upone the said Hendrie his face.......unlawit in V lib.

and, if a glass was not to hand, more unusual weapons were
sometimes available:

8th February 1639

And anent the complaint gevine be the said Johne Gairdner againis
the said Alexander Levingstoune for stryking of him wt ane stalfe or
golfeclub and blooding of him yrwt upone the face to the effusioune
of his bloode on the 2 day of february instant wtin the burgh of Falkirk.

Where the local golfers hit a ball with the club, rather than their
opponents, has not yet been discovered though a couple of entries
in the Session records suggest that the first Falkirk links were at the
Cleddens. No doubt the public executions which were also held
there from time to time provided some diversion for those golfers
waiting for the players ahead to clear the next green!

The picture that emerges from the crowded pages of the Court
Book is of a busy, even a bustling, small town which had obviously
made rapid strides in the relatively short period of its legitimate
burghhood. It was considerably larger with a population of between
one and two thousand living and working in a much more complex
network of streets, not very different from the town centre today.
A charter of 1645 mentions 'reparations and extensions about to
be made in the town of Falkirk', and certainly a good deal of
building work was undertaken from then on despite the unsettled
times. The High Street was, by then, established as the principal
thoroughfare, with what may have been the former main street
becoming as a consequence, the 'Back Raw'- now Manor Street.
That part of the High Street immediately to the west of the present
steeple became the town market place where the jail or tolbooth
stood, along with the symbol of burghal status, the mercat cross
and the official weighing machine or tron. Many street names
familiar today, Fleshmarket Close, Wooer (Weaver) Street, and
Baxters (Bakers) Wynd recall the trades of the old burgh, while
Lint Riggs, Bean Row and the Cow Wynd of course, remind us that
the new prosperity such as it was, derived in the main from

agriculture and would continue to do so for a century and a half. A number of new buildings were erected during this period; the Earl of Callendar himself had a new town house built just off the Kirk Wynd near its junction with the Back Raw and a new Tolbooth with a steeple was built in 1697 to replace the earlier one. The Lairds of Bantaskine, Westquarter and Rashiehill built substantial lodgings on the High Street and visitors to the town at the end of the century talk about a number of new stone lands or tenements under construction in the same area.

In this growing trading community the quality and quantity of what was brought forward for sale was a matter of constant concern to the baillies and the pages of the Barony Court Book contain many enactments on bread, ale, meat and meal and even shoes. Agents were deputed to visit the market and search out the 'blawne mutton and collapit flesche', or ensure that white bread was sold at 'ane unce for ane penny' and no more. We might these days envy Alexander Watt and John Warden of the Cow Wynd who were appointed as the official 'testeris of aill', duty bound to visit all the suppliers in Falkirk and ensure that their product was worth the fixed price of one shilling and eightpence! And tasters of the unofficial variety found themseles on the wrong end of the law. Witness the sad tale of John Gow and William Baillie who were collecting several hogsheads of claret from Falkirk's official port on the Carron at Abbotshaugh. Having 'ane inclination to taste the berrie they did break up ane of the hogsheids and did drink themselves drunk therewth'—according to the charge they managed to get through three gallons, and were fined thirty pounds Scots for their efforts!

Hard drinking was a common complaint among the fleshers of whom there were an astonishing number in Falkirk at the time. A great deal of mutton and beef must have been available for sale and this must throw doubt on the commonly held view that lowland Scots people existed on oatmeal and precious little else at this particular period. The fleshers were a constant source of concern for both Baron Court and Kirk Session. Sometimes it was their language which annoyed the elders:

November 1668

It was represented to the Session of the horrible and unchristian-like life of the fleshers in this town lived in profaining the Lord's name by cursing and swearing. Therfor the Session has appointed John Moir to wait upon the fleshmercat on Munday, James Sword upon Tuesday, John Mack upon Wednesday and Thomas Burn on Thursday, to remark the banners and swearers and to report.

One has visions of these devout agents listening in at the door of the market and cringing at every expletive from the unruly butchers, but continuing with their sacred duty nonetheless! More often it was the Court which had to deal with the countless assaults involving the fleshers, whose disdain for authority was typified by one John Stirling who was fined twenty pounds for saying that 'he caired not ane fart for any baillie in Falkirk'.

But the authorities efforts to maintain a safe and peaceful community went far beyond controlling the behaviour of the inhabitants of the burgh. External threats like the plague which visited the Falkirk area in late 1644 produced a swift response from both the civil and religious powers. In December of that year we find the Earl of Callendar writing to his Falkirk baillie urging immediate action to close up houses and guard others and to ensure that those confined are supplied with 'meill and coales'. Since contaminated clothing had to be destroyed, the Earl ordered his men to 'try what course cloath can be gottin in Falkirk at 2s or half a croune ane ell, and buy it, and cause all the taylzeours fall a making of four tailed coats and breiches.' Both Presbytery and Session deemed the arrival of the pestilence a divine punishment and special days of prayer and fasting were ordered. But more practical decisions were also taken which satsfied both spiritual and earthly requirements—'Banquittas, brydellies and nicht wakes were not decent when God is offendit with the land'. Later it was decreed that no shearers would be allowed in the town without an official pass. The plague stayed for fully two years in the town and there were many victims who were not permitted a burial in the kirkyard for fear that the pestilence would survive and return when lairs were opened. Instead they were carried outside the town to the common land and buried together in what were thereafter known as the Pest Graves. A stout stone wall was built round the spot on Graham's Muir to prevent cattle from eating the grass, but a more enlightened generation removed all traces the following century. The site lies at the junction of George Street and Russell

Street on the north-east corner and few of the inhabitants of the area are aware of its existence—perhaps it is just as well!

James Livingston's exile in Holland did not last long. Soon after the execution of Charles 1 in 1649, his young son agreed on Livingston's advice, to accept the conditions offered by the Scots, and become what they had always wanted—a 'covenanted King'. The Earl thought this new arrangement would restore him to favour especially as the formidable army of Cromwell was on its way north to punish the Scots for their renewed support of the Stewarts. But he was wrong. The unlawful 'engagement' was still roundly condemned and the forfeiture of his house and lands was confirmed by the Parliament. He was classified a 'malignant' and ordered out of Scotland. Three months later the Scottish army was shattered at Dunbar but only after a long argument and with severe reservations did the Estates finally agreed to allow the Earl to return and assist the country in her hour of great need.

Personal rivalry coupled with his previous record of vacillation prevented him from playing a leading role in the Scottish army and he was unable to return to Callendar House because the exclusion remained against him. He was therefore spared the immediate vengeance of Cromwell and his hardened Parliamentary army which came face to face with the new King and his followers near Linlithgow in the early summer of 1651. Advancing to meet them there, Cromwell's troops drew close to the Callendar castle of his old enemy James Livingston. What happened next is uncertain. One account suggests that Cromwell asked for, and was given, a solemn undertaking that the defenders of the castle would refrain from firing on the English troops as they passed by. In return the building and its occupants would be left alone. As soon as Cromwell's troops came within range, the Livingston guns opened up and the roundheads responded by turning back to punish the perfidious Scots. Other versions of the story have Cromwell and his men marching straight to Falkirk to begin the seige without pause for negotiation! Whatever the truth we do know that a detachment under General George Monck, Coldstream Guards, then known as Monck's Regiment—subjected the house or 'castle' to a considerable bombardment and its defences were blasted down by the superior firepower of the enemy. The castle was, of course, still the plain fortified building of Mary Stuart's time but it probably had crenellations and gunloops as well as a moat, drawbridge and

curtain barbican wall some distance in front of the building itself.
Despite this it proved no match for Monck's determined veterans,
among whom was one Cornet Baynes whose letter dated 19th July
1651 reports on the attack:

> From the camp near Kallender House we advanced again to Fawkirk
> near to Torwood. We have been here four nights. Upon Tuesday last
> about sunset after we had made a breach upon Kallendar House even
> in the face of the enemy we stormed it and lost a captain of foot, our
> gunner Robert Hargreave of your troop and 2 or 3 private soldiers.
> More were slain in the storm. We slew the enemy about 50 persons,
> and such as had quarter given them were most of them wounded. Little
> was taken from the house except horses and cattle of the country
> people.

One account suggests that James Livingston may have watched the
destruction of his home from the entrenchments of the Scottish
army but there was to be no swift revenge for him. The main armies
did not clash and the Scots withdrew to the Torwood and formed
a defensive line above the Carron crossing at Larbert.

In the immediate aftermath of the defeat, the town and even the
church were subjected to the privations inflicted when a large and
unfriendly army are in residence. Some accounts suggest that
horses were stabled in the kirkyard and that soldiers slept in the
nave of the church itself—the area of the town adjacent to the
glebe of the church, which is still known as the 'garrison' may well
date from this period. Cattle and sheep went to feed the hungry
troopers and many months after the departure of Cromwell's men,
locals were still asking for help from the church to offset their
losses. For a period the Government's Commander in Scotland,
General Monck, made his headquarters at Callendar House and
he may have began the repairs and restoration of the building
which had been so damaged in the encounter.

The final defeat of Charles 1 by Cromwell at Worcester in
September 1651 did not help James Livingston in his quest to
regain his estates. For the next five years he moved about the
country, sometimes living in 'his house in Pinkie', for several
months confined in Burntisland and Edinburgh Castles for sus-
pected contact with royalists and in Aberdeen on secret business
which may have involved the loyalist forces in the highlands. He

spent seven months in London in 1655 in an attempt to petition Cromwell directly to lift the sequestration on his Falkirk estates. In the end he was successful and early the following year, at the age of sixty he was at last restored to the House and lands of Callendar after an exile of nearly eight years. Throughout this period he seems to have retained the loyalty of his Falkirk followers and, according to the Court Book, the Falkirk baillies continued to exercise baronial power in his name. He found the house and estates in very poor condition and his financial affairs in disarray— according to the trustees who had held the estates, the Callendar income per annum was £1,554 and the debts £24,317! He began the process of restoration of both house and lands and spent much of the rest of his life in this task though he did sit in the Parliament from time to time. He was one of only fourteen noblemen who carried the coffin of the great Montrose to his place of honour in St Giles in May 1661.

The original Cross Well from 1681 with its 1817 replacement. *Drawings* Ian Scott.

One of his first acts in Falkirk was to establish a small refuge or 'hospital' for the aged which stood to the west of Lint Riggs, and tradition has also linked his name with the building of the Cross Well in the market place near the Tolbooth. As a reward for their loyalty, or so the story goes, the old Earl arranged for a line of water pipes made of hollow tree trunks jointed by lead, to be laid from his policies to the south of the town, to the High Street. There a large and handsome well-head of dressed stone was constructed, bearing the Livingston coat of arms, and, on one memorable day, the Earl arrived to hand over his gift to the people. One Victorian antiquarian with an eye for the romantic moment and a style to match, takes up the story:

> He caused his feuars to range themselves at the cross and after thanking them for the gallantry with which they had fought beside him, and reminding them of the many fields through which their fathers had followed his.....having filled a bicker from the pure well stream which was poured from the mouth of a sculptured lion, the grey haired baron stood up in his stirrups and drank off a quaich ' To the wives and Bairns o' Falkirk' giving them the well and all its fountains in present, forever.

......and presumably their nickname as well for 'Bairns' the inhabitants of the town certainly are, and have been for at least two centuries. Alas for the romantic, the accepted date for the opening of the well is 1681 several years after the death of James, and the arms on the well-head are those of his nephew Alexander who succeeded him around 1674. The original well-head shown in the drawing was demolished in the early 19th century and replaced by familiar roundal of ashlar which bears the date 1817. It is at present under repair but its return is promised soon.

Throughout the century when episcopalian and presbyterian held sway by turns, the changing fortunes appear to have provoked little open defiance in the town of Falkirk itself. While clergy of the wrong persuasion were elsewhere forced from their charges, successive ministers of the parish survived, although the tendancy of the masters and ministers to support episcopacy, and the preference of the people for a presbyterian settlement, must have created some real tension. In the early years of the century, for example, the minister Adam Bellenden, brother of the commendator Sir Lewis, was a staunch presbyterian whose opposition to the continued existence of bishops in the Scottish church, brought a brief suspension and a stern warning as to his future conduct. In keeping with the times he went on to experience a conversion, before becoming first Bishop of Dunblane and then of Aberdeen. Later, in the 1650s, after Cromwell's triumph, several people in Falkirk protested at the performance of their minister Mr Edward Wright whose episcopalian leanings were well known. Once again the suspension which followed was brief and the minister was soon restored to his pulpit. Maybe these relatively mild protests did not turn to violent opposition because the people feared retribution, but possibly the real impact of change on liturgy and church management at the local level was more limited than the stormy national disputes would suggest. Either way, most of the great movements seemed to impinge on Falkirk people only when the call came to arms once more or when soldiers of another power arrived to take over the town.

When James Livingston's adventurous life came to a peaceful end around 1674 he was close to his eightieth year. Although he left no legitimate heir he did not die childless for we have a record of one son, Sir Alexander Livingston of Dalderse and a daughter Lady Helenora Livingston of Bantaskin who were born over half a century before. But the new master of Callendar was his nephew Alexander, the second son of the Earl of Linlithgow, a passionate supporter of the protesting covenanters. The restoration of the Charles II had brought a steady return to the episcopal policies which had led to his father's deposition and many Scottish presbyterians took to the open fields to worship in the way they preferred. Presbytery records suggest that such conventicles were taking place within Falkirk parish with the open support of Lord Alexander. Government troops seized Callendar House in 1675 and again three years later when, according to one historian, 'the Falkirk mob rose in great fury and put the intruders to flight'. The following year Alexander's half brother the 3rd Earl of Linlithgow, who was, by contrast a strong royalist and episcopalian, marched through Falkirk with the celebrated Graham of Claverhouse, the 'Bonnie Dundee' of legend, on the way to the bloody slaughter of the covenanters at Bothwell Bridge.

The Government introduced new tests to ascertain the beliefs of people in positions of power and authority and when Alexander declined he was 'put to the horn' in July 1683, denounced at the mercat cross as a rebel and stripped of his baronial power. Two years later he died and was succeeded by Linlithgow's second son, also Alexander. He was, as one might expect, a staunch Episcopalian—once again the pendulum had moved, this time back to where it had been for most of the century.

Despite the sustained opposition of their latest Lord, the people of Falkirk parish seemed to welcome the final settlement which followed the deposing of the Catholic King, James II and his replacement by William of Orange in 1688. By the end of the century the whole episcopal system was effectively dead in Scotland and from then on the ministers in the Falkirk pulpit were confirmed presbyterians. A period of peace and quiet was what the growing burgh and its war weary population badly needed but when the new century dawned, it was very much the mixture as before.

CHAPTER 5

Cattle Trysts and Highland Armies

In 1695 the two Earldoms of Callendar and Linlithgow were combined once again, in the person of yet another James Livingston, whom fate had decreed would be the last Earl of Callendar His early years were marked by periods of crop failure and severe hardship throughout Scotland and the Falkirk area was no exception. The Kirk Session reported that 'the number of poor within the parish does dayly abound', and schemes to relieve growing poverty occupied much of their time. No class in the district was exempt from the impact and the elders found it difficult to raise money among the leading men of the parish or even call in the loans made over the years to various lairds and merchants. 'King Williams years' as these lean times came to be known, brought Falkirk's steady growth to an end for a time and prospects as the new century opened were decidedly grim.

The triumph of Presbyterianism brought new severity to the daily life of the people, already oppressed by the vagaries of nature. Puritanism returned with a vengeance and the Sabbath desecraters, fiddlers, dancers, and fornicators found themselves pursued with renewed vigour. Public repentance multiplied and the numbers banished from the parish increased. The earliest act of the new Minister in 1694, William Burnett, had been to complain about the pillar being too 'great a distance from the pulpit and so darkly situat'. Out it came into the open and business boomed! The old Kirk was in a poor state of repair and efforts by the Session to have the leading landowners, and the new Earl, do something about it came to nothing. By 1710 things were so severe that the Session ordered 'John Jervay, wright in Falkirk' to prop up one of the walls, and once again appealed for help to rescue the 'ruinous fabrick' of the church. Although he eventually agreed to this, James Livingston's thoughts were elsewhere.

Like most of his ancestors he was a Stewart loyalist and cherished hopes of a return to the throne for the exiled family of King James. He was involved at an early stage in the intrigue of the Earl of Mar to raise a Jacobite army and when the Stewart standard was raised in 1715 he was appointed a brigadier in command of a regiment of horse. He fought in the indecisive battle at Sherrifmuir with Falkirk men by his side, but the lack of a clear cut victory brought the Jacobite challenge to a swift end. Tradition has it that James returned to his house after the battle, but that a detachment of Government troopers arrived in Falkirk soon after to seek him out. Once again the loyal 'bairns' came to his rescue by delaying the soldiers at the mercat cross, with sticks and stones, thus allowing Earl James to escape to exile. With him went the Livingston dynasty for soon after he was attainted, his lands forfeited and the Earldoms of Linlithgow and Callendar extinguished. He died in France in 1725 and the York Buildings Company of London became the proprietors of his ancient house and land.

In 1723 Alexander Johnstone of Kirkland left a detailed description of the 'village of Falkirk' and the surrounding countryside in

The steeple and tolbooth erected in 1697. it was replaced by the present steeple in 1814. *Drawing* John Reid

the aftermath of the failed rebellion and the hasty departure of the leading landowner. Although his opinion confirms the general view that 'this place has suffered extremely' he describes the state of the town and its commerce in fulsome terms:

> This village has an excellent weekly market upon Thursday, where there is not only all kinds of vivars to be sold ..... a great abundance of pease and beans .... with a considerable meal market. There are very good houses here and yeards. I doubt not but this is as sweet a village considering all things, as is in Scotland!

He remarks particularly on the handsome Tolbooth with beautiful steeple, clock and bell, the well and pond in the centre of the village and the church—'a very considerable fabrick, finely re-paired within, with seats in a regular maner'.

Although the Livingston power was gone, the presence of the family remained and still had one last dramatic part to play in the story of Callendar and Falkirk. In 1721 Lady Ann Livingston daughter of the exiled James was allowed by the York Buildings Company to rent the house and lands formerly held by her family, on a twenty-nine year lease. She had earlier married William Boyd, Earl of Kilmarnock and he now took up residence in Callendar House and more or less assumed the role of first citizen. He was, for example, the Grand Master of the Falkirk Lodge of Free Masons for several years and acted as principal landowner in dealing with the Parish Church. Though his loyalty seemed to lie initially with the Government and ruling Hanovarians, whom he and his family had supported in 1715, his wife was, like her Livingston forebears, an unrepentant Jacobite. When the opportunity came to demonstr-ate the loyalty she did not fail the test, but her dogged adherence to a lost cause brought her dynasty crashing down in the wake of Prince Charlie's rising in 1745.

Things began well enough. The 'young pretender' passed the night in Callendar House in September of that year on his way to a triumph at Prestonpans and a rapturous reception in Edinburgh. Among the ladies who surrounded the handsome chevalier in his happy days in the capital, Lady Ann was said to be the most dazzling and beautiful! But the fateful march south to Derby and the retreat back to Scotland signalled the beginning of the end of the Stewart cause. As ever, Falkirk lay in the path of both Jacobite and Hanovarian armies as they moved northwards towards the stronghold of Stirling Castle.

In January 1746 an opportunity to deliver a counter blow against the pursuing Government forces presented itself. General Henry Hawley in command of nearly nine thousand men had made camp in Falkirk on land to the west of the town from Hope Street down towards the present Dollar Park. The Jacobite commanders besieging Stirling Castle decided that a carefully planned attack might rout the redcoats and begin a revival in the fortunes of their luckless Prince. On January 17th aided by Sir Archibald Primrose of Dunipace—under duress, or so he claimed at his subsequent trial—the highland armies moved from Plean in a southward circle across the rivers Carron and Bonny towards the south muir of Falkirk. By late afternoon the high ground was held by over eight thousand men, highland infantry from all the major clans supported by cavalry of the lowland Jacobite gentry. The Earl of

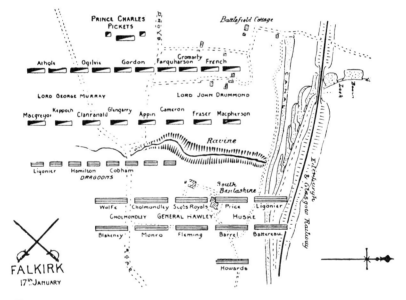

The positions of the Government and Jacobite armies at the Second Battle of Falkirk on 17th January 1746. This particular version of the battle plan was made in the 19th century by one of the Wilson family of South Bantaskine and shows the battle ground set against the layout of the estate in the mid Victorian period with the roads, railway and Union Canal.

Kilmarnock now 'out with the rebels' and his Falkirk tenants were among them.

Two miles away in Callendar House Lady Ann was entertaining the unsuspecting Hawley, who, on hearing the bad news, rose from the table in some disarray according to one account, found his horse and galloped towards his army to begin a belated response.

The stained glass windows from the Howgate centre showing Lord George Murray, Bonnie Prince Charlie and Lord John Drummond. They were originally made for South Bantaskine House around 1860.

Chevalier Johnstone was with the Prince and he later recalled the scene as the dragoons of Cobham, Ligonier and Hamilton led the Government forces up Maggie Woods Loan towards the Jacobite positions in the foulest winter weather. After receiving a blast of fire from the highland lines which killed eighty men, the cavalry charged forward:

> The most singular and extraordinary combat immediately followed. The Highlanders, stretched on the ground, thrust their dirks into the bellies of the horses. Some seized the riders by their clothes, dragged them down, and stabbed them with their dirks; several, again, used their pistols, but few of them had sufficient space to handle their swords The resistance of the Highlanders was so incredibly obstinate that the English, after having been for some time engaged pell-mell with them in their ranks were at length repulsed and forced to retire.

It was a ferocious clash with the highlanders charging hard downhill towards their fleeing enemy and though the left wing fared less well and confusion reigned for a time, the overall outcome was a near complete Jacobite victory. Government forces fled in disarray from the town, setting fire to their tents and abandoning great quantities of equipment. Within a few hours three columns of highland soldiers entered through the town ports—Lord George Murray by Roberts Wynd, Lord John Drummond by the Cow Wynd and Cameron of Lochiel by the West Port. A century later the event was commemorated in the beautiful stained glass windows of South Bantaskine House on whose land the battle was fought. Now appropriately enough they grace the new shopping centre not far from the point where the Prince's soldiers entered the town and where he spent several nights in the 'great lodging', the former home of Livingston of Westquarter.

Casualties were high among the redcoats with between three and four hundred killed and many more taken prisoner. The Jacobite losses were less, some say as few as forty men. As with the other battle centuries before, great pits were dug the following day and the naked bodies, stripped bare in the night by the country people or victorious clansmen, were laid to rest. A little copse beside Dumyat Drive is thought to mark one of these places and another lay close to the present High Station. Several prominent people were buried in the Falkirk churchyard including Colonel Robert

William Boyd, Earl of Kilmarnock, executed in 1746 and the Battle of Falkirk monument erected in 1927. *Photograph Roy Earle.*

Munro and his brother Dr Duncan Munro cut down by the Camerons in the rout after brave resistance, and the young officer William Edmonstone of Cambuswallace. The Church itself along with the tolbooth and the cellars of Callendar House were used to hold the prisoners. Little depredation took place in the town and an old tradition suggests that the highlanders found the product of the ale and porter brewery founded several years before very much to their liking! The site of the battle on the south muir is today marked by an obelisk unveiled by the Duke of Atholl in 1927. It is a modest memorial of such a great encounter, the last time the famous 'highland charge' carried the day. A more chilling reminder of the battle can be found in the many eye witness accounts which survive. Among the most graphic was that of Chevalier Johnstone who was sent with a sergeant and twenty men to guard the captured cannons on the battlefield:

> The sergeant carried a lantern; but the light was soon extinguished, and by that accident we immediately lost our way, and wandered a long time at the foot of the hill, among heaps of dead bodies, which their whiteness rendered visible. To add to the disagreeableness of our situation from the horror of the scene, the wind and the rain were full in our faces. I even remarked a trembling and strong agitation in my horse, which constantly shook when it was forced to put its feet on the heaps of dead bodies and to climb over them.....on my return to Falkirk I felt myself relieved from an oppressive burden: but the horrid spectacle I had witnessed was for a long time, fresh in my mind.

Only once more would British soil witness such carnage and that just three months later on Drumossie Moor at Culloden. On that day Kilmarnock was taken, as the Jacobite cause perished. In August he was beheaded on Towerhill in London and Lady Ann, retreating in abject misery to her husband's family home, lay in a blackened room and 'wept herself blind before dying of grief'.

But the jaunty highland troops who left Falkirk a few days after the battle had no thoughts of Culloden or defeat but like their Prince, they were in high spirits and full of optimism. They were not the first highlanders to spend time in Falkirk of course and as the century wore on many more of their fellows would make the town their autumn home as Falkirk trysts grew in size and importance to become the greatest cattle fairs in Europe. For centuries the cattle of the highland glens had found a ready market in the lowlands where arable farming predominated. Increasingly buyers from England too made the long journey north to meet and deal with the highland drovers whose sturdy kyloe had walked hundreds of miles over grassy drove roads to the great market of Crieff. It was probably the continued growth in demand from the south after the union with England in 1707 which prompted landowners in the Falkirk district to organise the first cattle markets which sixty years later would eclipse all others in Scotland.

A large area of common land on Redding muir, acquired by the Dukes of Hamilton, from the Bellendens in the aftermath of the Reformation, became the site of the earliest trysts. Unlike the weekly town markets, the annual meetings of buyers and sellers of cattle, sheep and horses had no legal standing. The owners of the land simply advertised the availability of the ground for such meetings and slowly, over many decades, the numbers of livestock on offer increased as news spread by word of mouth. The earliest Falkirk record dates from 1717 and in it the Duke of Hamilton—who also held the title of Lord Polmont—sets tolls for the cattle, horses and sheep arriving for sale at Redding. One account suggests that the profits in the early years did not reach the coffers of the noble proprietor, since it had been 'eaten and drunken by the former factor, baillie and clerk'.

Despite the obvious difficulties encountered by highlanders during the Jacobite rising the trysts continued to function but a greater threat came with the agricultural reforms which swept the country from the middle of the 18th century. Everywhere great areas of common land were being subdivided and brought under cultivation and in 1761 the feuars petitioned the courts to allow the division and allocation of the commonty of Reddingrigmuir and Whitesiderigmuir. Despite an eleven year fight by the Duke to preserve the trysts, and his income from them, the courts ruled for the feuars and in the early 1770s the great fair had moved to a second location to the south-west of the town at Roughcastle.

But if the enclosure of land forced the move to a new site in Falkirk the same reason lay behind the massive increase in business which appeared at the same period. The great Michaelmas fair held in Crieff each October where as many as 30,000 head of cattle were offered for sale began to decline as more of the stances were lost. From then on an October fair developed at Roughcastle along with those held in August and September. This became the pattern for the next century with the second Tuesday of each month the official sale day.

The great gathering of Gaels in a lowland town prompted the Highland Society of London to establish a great piping competition at Falkirk tryst in 1781 and it was held there for several years before moving eventually to Edinburgh. But the construction of the Forth and Clyde canal from 1768 onwards caused considerable difficulties for the drovers who had to negotiate yet another obstacle in their journey southwards. By 1785 the Falkirk tryst was once more on the move this time north of the canal and the river Carron into the parish of Larbert. The site at Stenhousemuir housed the trysts from then on until the last decades of the 19th century and are still home to the last remnants of the great gathering—the annual fair and sideshows.

At their height the trysts were a sensational sight with as many as 150,000 cattle, sheep and horses arriving in great streams from all corners of Scotland and settling in the fields with their drovers, 'great stalwart, hirsute men, shaggy uncultured and wild', perhaps as many as two thousand with ponies and dogs, sleeping in the open or in portable bivouacs. From the borders and from England hundreds of buyers descended on the area moving among the animals on horseback sealing a bargain here and spurning an offer there. The bustle and clamour of the market was remarked on by many observers who came to marvel at the scene. One thought it 'a scene to which certainly Great Britain perhaps even the whole world does not afford a parallel'. Supporting the buyers and the sellers was a remarkable tented village of banks, shops and taverns offering all manner of services to the dealers.

> Many kindle fires at the ends of their tents over which cooking is briskly carried on. Broth is made in considerable quantities and meets a ready sale. As most of the purchasers are paid in these tents, they are constantly filled and surrounded with a mixed multitude of cattle dealers, fishers, drovers, auctioneers, pedlars, jugglers, gamblers, itinerant fruit merchants, ballad singers and beggars. What an indescribable clamour prevails in most of these parti-coloured abodes.

Hundreds of thousands of pounds was paid over the counters of these temporary Banks during each tryst day and the impact on the local economy must have been very significant. In the 1760s for example one dealer arrived in the town from England with a Royal Bank credit note allowing him to spend up to £2000—the average price for one cow in that period was less than £2! By the end of the 18th Century upwards of half a million pounds was changing hands at the three trysts.

And they continued to grow through the first half of the 19th Century until the arrival of the railways made it possible for dealers to buy off the hill and sellers to transport south on wheels. By then the availability of open ground en route from the hills to Falkirk was decreasing and the fatter, carefully bred and cosseted cattle were less able to take the long walk to market. The tryst did continue but the numbers of livestock steadily declined until by 1900 the great markets were all but dead. One old man living in the town as a boy in the 1890s recalls that even in decline the arrival of the drovers in town was a sight to behold:

The first William Forbes of Callendar from the painting by Raeburn which once hung in the morning room at Callendar House.

Callendar House in 1789 not long after it was purchased by William Forbes.

We could hear the bellowing of the cattle and the bleating of the sheep and goats ... we watched them squeezing their way through the Kirk Wynd which was then as narrow as Roberts Wynd. When we got to Grahams Road there were as far as the eye could see, droves of livestock. We were afraid of the Highland drovers who were wild looking, unkempt crowd of raggimuffins who carried a roll of canvas on their shoulders for their tents, and billy-cans dangling from a piece of string. They were gesturing with their sticks and shouting in Gaelic at their long haired cattle with big long wide horns and wild eyes.

The failed Jacobite rising of 1746 was little more than a memory when the last Livingston house and lands were placed on the open market in 1783. With peaceful times long restored and families no longer subject to the stain of disloyalty, the habit of allowing them to purchase their ancestral lands unchallenged had developed. When the Livingston property was offered in three lots—Callendar, Almond and Carmuirs, it was expected that the same gentleman's agreement would apply. But they did not reckon with the formidable William Forbes. An Aberdeenshire merchant, Forbes had made a fortune in London by providing copper sheathing for the hulls of wooden ships. Now, as was the style, he sought to use his new wealth to buy into landed society. If he was aware of the special arrangements he did not allow the thought to divert him from his course. On all three lots he outbid his Livingston rival, the Earl of Errol, offering a total of nearly £90,000. When challenged by the selling agents to establish his bonefides as a purchaser he is said to have handed over a £100,000 note from the Bank of England! That will do nicely, Sir, was no doubt the reply and soon the Forbes influence was being felt throughout the town and district. It was the start of almost two centuries of power for the family, quite different in nature from that of the feudal Livingston Lords, but just as significant in terms of shaping the destiny of the town and its people.

A decade later the Minister of Falkirk Parish, Dr James Wilson described the state of agriculture in his entry for the famous Statistical Account of Scotland. 'Almost the whole of these estates,' he reported 'is now enclosed and subdivided—the ridges are straightened and the wet parts drained'. New leases required tenants to follow certain practices including proper rotations and liming of soil, and these who would not accept were effectively removed from the land. Such dislocation provoked reaction and it is evident that the positive action of William Forbes did not win him many friends in the area in these early years. One story has

Copper bottom's retreat, or a View of Carron Work!!!

Copperbottom's Retreat, by John Kay, published in 1837. It shows William Forbes fleeting from Callendar House thinking the building is on fire. The flames are actually from the great Carron Ironworks.

William returning to Callendar House from the south, seeing it apparently on fire and fleeing from what he took to be the revenge of disgruntled former tenants. It turned out to be no more than the fiery glow from the mighty furnaces of Carron Ironworks which had been established some thirty years earlier. Kay's famous portrait shows 'Copperbottom'—he had brought the nickname from London with him—fleeing in terror!

According to Wilson's account the population of the town in 1797 was 3,892 including 18 bakers, 22 grocers, one physician, five surgeons, two druggists and four clock and watchmakers! He had a good deal to say about the autumn trysts but reserved his most fulsome praise for two major developments which taken together would totally transform the district. The establishment of the ironworks at Carron in 1759 and the cutting of the 'great canal' from Forth to Clyde a decade later signalled the start of the industrial revolution in Scotland. The birth crucible of the nation in that first iron age fourteen hundred years before was once again the place where the new Scotland was shaped and formed. For fifty years afterwards the town and district remained essentially agricultural but the growing seeds of a new industrial future were already firmly established before the 18th century came to an end.

CHAPTER 6

A New Age of Iron

On the 15th June 1759 the Birmingham industrialist Samuel Garbett wrote to his Scottish partner William Cadell in Cockenzie. "Dr. Roebuck and I", he said, "think Carron Water is a situation infinitely preferable to all others". It is arguably the most important letter written in the history of the Falkirk district for the direct consequence was the establishment of the iron founding industry which dominated the lives of the people for well over two hundred years. Britain was at war with France yet again and imports of iron from the continent were seriously disrupted at a time when demand for munitions was greatly increased. Garbett and his partners believed that the central valley of Scotland offered the perfect location for a new, large scale works for smelting iron from local ore. Dr. John Roebuck, a medical man from Sheffield was already in partnership with Garbett making chemicals at Prestonpans and Cadell was a wealthy merchant with an established timber shipping and exporting business. He wanted to site the new venture near his properties in East Lothian but the others, especially Roebuck, much preferred land on the north bank of the Carron. There was iron ore available at Bo'ness and limestone supplies not far away in Maddiston and across the river near Dysart and Limekilns. Although timber would have to be brought from the highlands for conversion to charcoal there was an almost unlimited supply of coal which the farsighted businessmen knew would in the form of coke, eventually replace charcoal as the principal fuel for the smelters.

Above all there were the two rivers, Carron and Forth providing relatively easy access for raw materials and for the export of finished products and, equally importantly, offering water power to drive the bellows for the blast and the hammers of the forge. A company was formed with twenty-four £500 shares, 6 each to Garbett and Roebuck and the other 12 held by Roebuck's three brothers and Cadell and his son William who was appointed first Manager. Fourteen acres of land were feued from Sir Michael Bruce of

Stenhouse, the destroyer of Arthur's Oon, still trying to raise enough money to provide for his large family. Skilled workmen and special equipment were brought to Scotland from England and construction work began in the autumn of 1759.

There is a tradition fostered by the company over the years that iron was produced on the first day of 1760. We are told that in the presence of many visitors, Dr. Roebuck pierced the furnace breast allowing the stream of molten iron to fill the sand beds spread out beside the furnace. One observer remembered that "the cheers from the assembled guests were deafening and when they had subsided, Mr. Cadell called for a bumper to the works—'long years of prosperity to Carron and Dr. Roebuck'." The following day, we are told, the visitors returned to watch the iron converted into bars then forged into nails which were given out as souveniers to those present. If this happy event did indeed take place it was certainly not on the 1st January 1760 for it was several months before the works were capable of producing any iron far less the blast furnace product described in the story. The truth is that an air furnace was commissioned in March of the same year and the first iron was used to produce cannonballs. The first blast furnace was ready towards the end of the year and tapped on Boxing Day 26th December 1760. A year later a second furnace was commissioned and along with forges and rolling and boring mills gave the partners all the basic facilities they required to become a major force in the British iron industry.

It had been the demand for ordnance in the form of guns and cannonballs which had inspired the establishment of the works and the partners soon began to produce cannons in a variety of sizes for both the admiralty and the war office. The workers were for the most part brought from England and the works were dubbed the English foundry by the locals who appeared to resent the presence of their southern neighbours! If the following account is to be believed then more than angry words were exchanged:

> a sharp skirmish between some countrymen who were mending the highways and a parcel of the English workmen belonging to the Carron Iron Factory. The origin of the quarrel was some reflections thrown by the workers against Scotland and its inhabitants which the country fellows nobly resented...it quickly became a kind of national quarrel and reinforcements continually arriving to both sides.

From the outset the power of the River Carron was crucial. The infamous Stenhouse damhead rebuilt after the stones of Arthur's O'on were swept away, fed water to the Bruce Mill close to new works. It was not powerful enough to work the bellows for the blast or drive the forging hammers, and at an early stage the Furnace lade was constructed which drew water from the river a mile or so away near Larbert Church and fed a small reservoir adjacent to the works. Within twenty years this had been augmented by two much larger areas of water to create the familiar 'Carron dams' on which the works was to depend for so long. Giant bellows of wood and leather provided the air for the first two blast furnaces but by 1766 when the next two were commissioned, a water powered blowing machine devised by the famous engineer John Smeaton was installed.

Despite very severe problems in producing ordnance of a standard acceptable to the authorities and frequent financial difficulties, the ironworks grew at a phenomenal rate. By 1762 Roebuck had patented a process which used coked coal as the fuel and the laird of Quarrol, Thomas Dundas, had agreed to sell the company eighty tons of coal each week at 4/6 per ton from his two existing pits but eventually the company leased these from him and sunk a further four of their own. James Bruce the Abyssinian explorer, accepted £250 as an annual rent for the coal from his Kinnaird estate plus ten per cent of the value of the coal extracted. Later on the Duke of Hamilton's coal from Brightons and the collieries on former Livingston lands of Callendar and Shieldhill began supplying the works. Coal was carted through Falkirk almost continuously from then on, down the Cow Wynd, which from the late 1700s was known as Coal Heugh Road, along the High Street and then out over the long open road through Grahamston and Bainsford to Carron.

And it was the continuous search for new sources of fuel which brought the partners into contact with the Glasgow engineer James Watt. Roebuck had acquired the right to mine coal at Kinneil, Bo'ness as a personal investment but the colliery soon experienced difficulty with flood water which the available beam engine could not handle. He thought that Watt's ideas for increasing the efficiency of the engine might solve the problem. The works attempted with only limited success to cast and bore cylinders to Watt's specification and for several years he worked at Kinneil under

Roebuck's patronage. An engine was produced in March 1766 but it was not satisfactory and soon after Roebuck's personal financial difficulties led him to sell his share in the invention to Matthew Boulton of Birmingham. Watt moved south to continue his work in 1773 but long before then Roebuck's bankrupcy had ended his interest in Carron.

In 1768 Garbett's son-in-law Charles Gascoigne took over as Manager from Cadell and soon he was far more powerful than any of the partners. Having helped oust the bankrupt Roebuck he outmanoeuvred the Cadells and pushed Garbett into a relatively minor role in the Company's affairs. With considerable skill he reorganised Carron's financial structure to ensure that the rapid expansion was adequately funded and in 1773 managed the incorporation of Carron Company under a Royal Charter. For nearly twenty years he dominated the firm and it was in no small measure due to his skill and ruthlessness that Carron survived.

It was under his influence, for example, that the Company's most famous product was born in 1778. This naval gun which was eventually called the Carronade, had a very large calibre in comparison to its other dimensions and because it was relatively short it could be recharged and fired again much more quickly. Its effect

The yard at Carron Works in the mid 19th century. The bell on the top of the triangle was used to signal the start and end of the working day.

at close quarters was said to be devastating and it soon overcame the reluctance of the Admiralty to trust the unreliable guns from Carron. The Carronade was probably the brainchild of General Robert Melville, but improved and developed by the famous Patrick Miller under Gascoigne's direction. Indeed it was known during development as the Gasconade but by the time it was put on the market its famous name was established. The gun could fire almost four times the weight delivered in one shot by conventional naval guns and it was soon in demand by navies all over Europe. By 1791 they were mounted on 429 British ships and were being exported to Russia, Denmark and Spain. Visitors flocked to the works which were rapidly gaining the reputation as one of the world's wonders with the flashing fires of the furnace, lighting the sky above for miles around. In 1784 the French Royal Commissioner of Mines, Barthelemy Faujas de St Fond recorded his amazement at the scene which greeted him in the parts of the works he was allowed to see:

> He conducted us at first to an immense yard—covered with cannons, mortars, bombs, balls—amidst these machines of war these terrible instruments of death, gigantic cranes, capstans of every kind, levers and assemblages of pulleys. Under the sheds we saw several rows of rampart cannon siege guns and field pieces, destined for Russia.

But more than the products it was the process which impressed him most of all.

> When one observes from some way off—so many sheaves of flame darting to a great height above the high furnace and at the same time hears the noise of the heavy hammers as they strike on resounding anvils, mingled with the sharp whistling of the blast pumps, one doubts whether he is not at the foot of a volcano in eruption.

But the 'terrible instruments of death' were far from the only product cast or hammered out beneath the towering forty-five foot furnaces—sugar boilers for the West Indies, stoves of every kind, grates, kitchen ranges, kettles, tea pots, frying pans, spades, hoes, hinges, and bolts. This combination of domestic and agricultural tools and equipment, with the guns and mortars for the navies and armies of the world was a formula that was to serve Carron well in war and peace for more than two hundred years.

Perhaps the most remarkable aspect of the Carron story in those early decades was its continued growth against a background of financial crises, constant material and power shortages, product failure, labour disputes, complex legal arguments with unhelpful local lairds, and bitter personal rivalry among the partners. The sheer scale of the demand for iron products in Britain and beyond, overcame the most serious of impediments and by the end of the century the Company was strong and prosperous. Its influence extended to every aspect of the life of Falkirk district; it became a leading heritor in the parishes of Larbert and Falkirk and a powerful voice in the decisions which shaped the economic, social, religious and political future of the area.

But it was the physical impact of such a huge undertaking on the locality which was more immediate. Villages were born peopled by colliers from Shropshire and masons, wrights, and moulders from Derby. Agricultural workers cast adrift by enclosure and improvement on the land were drawn by the magnet of regular employment to labour alongside the skilled men from the south. Ancient mills along the length of the Carron were bought up and, where the miller once ground oats and barley, fresh castings were finished and charcoal dust blackened the ancient stones. Within a year, over six hundred men were employed and a decade later it was said by one visitor to be over 1100. Working and living conditions were deplorable even by 18th Century standards. The Scottish colliers in particular still suffered from their legal status as bonded labour, tied to their pit and employer to be bought or sold like so many wooden props or lengths of waggon rail. The squalor in which they and their families were forced to live, so debased and dehumanised them as to provoke all manner of disputes, frequent drunkenness and violence, widespread theft and even full scale rioting. On several occasions during the early years, troops were called in by the managers to put down the disturbances—the prevailing philosophy of the times regarded concern and compassion as weaknesses likely to provoke idleness and lead the firm to financial ruin. In this the managers regretted the need to depend on the 'undeserving Scots' rather than on the English who were 'sober and commendable and they live in very decent fashion'.

The spirit of the times which had inspired the Carron venture gave rise to an explosion of enterprise across Scotland and led directly to renewed proposals to cut a waterway from the Forth to the Clyde in the 1760s. The short neck of land between the Irish and North Seas which the Romans had crossed with their great wall had been identified as early as the 1660s as the ideal place for a canal but it was not until economic and social conditions were right a century later that the work was begun. In 1762 the great engineer Robert McKell surveyed a route on behalf of a group of Glasgow merchants and shortly afterwards John Smeaton was invited by the Board of Trustees for the Encouragement of Fisheries, Manufactures and Improvements in Scotland to produce an alternative version which was the one finally adopted. Smeaton's proposal, modified in several ways after it was first produced, envisaged a 35 mile canal over fifty feet wide and seven feet deep from an eastern terminus where the Carron joined the Forth, to the Clyde near Bowling. A series of locks would carry the barges across the carse immediately north and west of Falkirk, from Middlefield to Bainsford and on through Camelon to Bonnybridge. From there a further four locks would lift the canal up to its highest point at Wyndford Lock near Castlecary over 150 feet above the sea. Thereafter it was stepped down through a further 19 locks across to the Clyde north of Glasgow. A cut from the canal into the city would ensure that the produce of the east coast would have a path to the rapidly expanding commercial heart of the west coast.

In 1767 a public company was formed with fifteen hundred £100 shares subscribed to by the most powerful and influential figures in the land. There were six Dukes and seventeen Earls, as well as the Lord Provosts of both Edinburgh and Glasgow, but by far the biggest single shareholder was Sir Lawrence Dundas of West Kerse with £10,000 worth of stock. The canal would begin its journey on his land and, as a result, he stood to gain in every way from its success. Parliament approved the proposal in 1768 and in the same year the work began.

It was a colossal undertaking, the greatest civil engineering project in Scotland since the Roman builders completed the Antonine Wall over the same ground over 1600 years before. Smeaton was appointed as chief engineer with a salary of £500 and Robert McKell, his assistant, was paid £375. These were princely sums in the mid 18th Century when one of the thousand men engaged to dig the canal was to be paid less than one shilling per day. McKell certainly earned his pay for he was in charge of the day-to-day work—searching out and buying timber, stone and clay, engaging skilled masons and bridge builders as well as scores of untried labourers. These navigators or 'navvies' who by all accounts, fought, drank and dug themselves from Falkirk all the way to the Clyde were not the easiest of workforces and McKell must have envied his Roman predecessors with military discipline available to keep their building squads in line!

One can hardly imagine the impact on a small town of the arrival of these huge armies of workmen, living in temporary accommodation and disrupting the life and disturbing the peace of the inhabitants like the soldiers of previous centuries. Such annoyance no doubt contributed to the hostility shown by locals to the whole project, but the real reason was the threat to the livelihood of the carters of the district represented by the canals. The arrival of Carron ironworks had increased the number of carters in the Falkirk area from four to over a hundred and now the canal looked likely to deprive them of their new found prosperity. Canal Company records report regular vandalism, dams and locks destroyed, equipment stolen, and workers attacked. Even worse was the breaking down of the top lockgate at Lock 16 in Camelon which released four miles of water between there and Lock 17 at Castlecary! By 1770 over 1500 men were working and the Canal had covered over fourteen miles. By 1775 the canal was completed as far as Stockingfield near Kirkintilloch and there was water in most of the eastern end so that trading along this part could begin. Financial difficulties delayed the completion of the final stretch until July 1790 when a ceremonial hogshead of Forth water was poured into the Clyde near Bowling. By then developments were already underway with small workshops and warehouses, tile works, timber yards and coal stores established along the length of the canal from the new village of Grangemouth in the east to Camelon and Bonnybridge in the west. More than any other development the cutting of the canal transformed Falkirk from the market town of the carse to a centre of industry with a wide range of new manufacturing activities and a growing population.

More and more vessels which had once used the established port of Bo'ness now landed raw materials and finished goods at Grangemouth, where they were loaded onto barges for the journey west. In the opposite direction came the imported goods of the great Glasgow merchants for onward transmission from the Forth to the rest of Britain and Europe. Initially goods were moved on horsedrawn barges but the inventive genius of the age soon found an outlet in the harnessing of steam power to the task. In 1789 Patrick Miller of Dalswinton whose involvement with the Carronade has already been noted, brought his 60 foot paddle boat The Experiment to the canal west of Lock 16 where there was a clear four mile run free of locks. It was fitted with a steam engine designed by William Symington of Wanlockhead and made in Carron. After several unsuccessful attempts during which Millar began to lose faith in the whole idea of steam navigation, The Experiment did finally sail on the canal on 25th December 1789. Miller was absent and he refused to support the venture further.

A decade later the sheer volume of shipping trying to use the completed canal led the Canal Company to think once again about the possibility of steam tugs. Lord Thomas Dundas, son of Sir Lawrence was by then the Governor of the Company and early in 1800 he asked Symington who was once again working at Wanlockhead, to design a new engine. The following year, a wooden hulled craft, probably designed by Captain John Schank

William Symington's *Charlotte Dundas*, claimed by many as the world's first practical steam powered boat.

of the Royal Navy and certainly fitted with Symington's steam engine was built by Alexander Hart of Grangemouth and launched with the name Charlotte Dundas. Contemporary reports suggested that the 58 foot by 18 foot boat had successful tests on the canal but the project was expensive and not without serious technical problems. In 1803 a second boat, probably also called Charlotte Dundas, was built to a modified design with an improved engine. Early the following year Symington tested the boat along the whole length of the canal and on 28th March witnessed by a number of important guests, the boat towed two large barges weighting some 130 tons a total a distance of 18½ miles in just over nine hours. It was generally regarded as a satisfactory if not spectacular performance but the fears of the Company that the boats would damage the banks of the canal persisted and the project, and Symington, were eventually abandoned. The boat served as a dredger before it finally rotted away at Tophill near Lock 10. Symington himself became the manager of Falkirk's Callendar Colliery for several years and lived in Kinnaird House, Larbert. He died in near poverty in London in 1831 aged just sixty eight. His work preceded that of Henry Bell and Robert Fulton and he is entitled to be remembered as the father of steam navigation, though it was many years before steam powered boats sailed on the Great Canal.

In the same year as the Forth and Clyde was completed the scarcity of coal in the capital led the Edinburgh city fathers to look towards the rich Lanarkshire coalfields for future supplies. The advantages of a waterway linking the city to the west was obvious and several possible routes were surveyed between 1793 and 1797 by distinguished engineers including John Rennie and Robert Whitworth. Involvement in the French wars delayed the project and when planning was resumed in 1813 a further plan by Hugh Baird was commissioned. This envisaged a line linking Edinburgh and Falkirk, where the two canals would join together. Despite many reservations from those who preferred an independent waterway from Edinburgh to Lanarkshire, the plan was eventually accepted. Work began in Edinburgh in March 1818 and continued, following the contours of the land right through to Falkirk, a total distance of 31 miles. Where valleys lay in its path great aqueducts were built such as the twelve mighty arches of the Avon aqueduct over eighty feet above the river and stretching for 900 feet. But the barriers were not always physical. The Forbes family of Callendar went to extraordinary lengths to ensure that the canal would not be visible from their estates. The campaign of opposition included producing a print and plan showing the effects of the development which was sent to every Member of Parliament in Britain. It was successful and engineers were forced to cut a 690 yard tunnel, possibly the oldest in the land, under Prospect Hill. This involved blasting and digging through solid rock, and the 'dark tunnel' as it is known remains a marvel even in this high technology age. The squads of navvies engaged in digging and lining the channel for over thirty-one miles were the same hard drinking, hard living gangs of displaced workers from the highlands and later from Ireland who had already made the Great Canal and would one day drive the railways across the length and breadth of the land. One observer was at least as concerned about their behaviour as he was impressed by the techniques involved. Writing from Falkirk to New York in September 20th 1818 he describes the project:

> their is a Cannal going throu from Falkirk to Edinburgh and they are cutting a tunal belaw grany from west side of our moar all the way to the glen burn about half a mill ..... they sunk pits about 100 yards from each other to the level of the cannal and then cut east and west till they met below taking all the stuff up by windlasts .....a great deal of Irish men came over and is employed at it and several accident has happened at it and 2 was killed by the face of the brea faling down on them.... few of our countrymen is at it as in general they cannot stand the work ..... they are mostly irish young men and a bad set they are.

Lock 16 at Camelon where the two canals, the Forth and Clyde and the Union joined together.

At the Falkirk end of the canal a flight of eleven locks bridged the gap to Lock 16 on the Forth and Clyde at Camelon where a basin was constructed at the junction. The whole expensive project with its aqueducts and over-bridges, linking locks and half-mile tunnel was completed in 1822 when the city centres of Glasgow and Edinburgh, and the estuaries of the two great rivers were joined at last in a waterway system which was almost as important as a symbol of man's ability to overcome and tame the natural world, as it was an element in the economic development of the nation.

If the carriage of coal and lime, iron ore and Baltic grain, tobacco and woolen plaids, earned the shareholders dividends and fired the industrial revolution, the canals also linked communities and offered passengers the opportunity of seeing their country in a way that had not been possible in the past. As early as 1822 a traveller's guide to the Edinburgh to Glasgow journey was pro-duced, pointing out the sights to be seen to north and south of both canals—the forest of masts at the new port of Grangemouth, the elegant villas and 'gentlemen's seats' and parklands, new church buildings and the flaming furnaces of Carron. It explained how passengers would disembark at Falkirk and walk the few hundred yards down to the basin and partake of refreshment at the new Union Inn while the barges passed through the chain of locks and basins ready for embarkation and a renewed journey to Bonnybridge and the west.

But the Union Canal as it came to be known was never as successful as the Forth and Clyde which remained the Great Canal in every way. The coming of the railways in the mid century changed everything but the Forth and Clyde especially continued as a key route for shipping, goods and passengers, remaining financially sound until the early years of this century. Thereafter the decline accelerated and in 1933 the section linking the two canals was abandoned and the locks filled in. In the early 1960s an Act of Parliament closed the canals and in 1966 the eastern end of the Forth and Clyde, from Grangemouth to Middlefield, was filled in. Despite the neglect of the intervening years both canals remain not only as a tangible link with the past but as assets which might yet be exploited once again for the benefit of the people of the district.

Ironically in the light of future developments, it was the canals that first brought railway locomotives to the district. In 1838 at the

Union Canal terminus at Causewayend a line of coal trucks from Airdrie arrived along the Slamannan Railway. By all accounts a goodly crowd walked from the town to see the iron horse enter the district for the first time—now the servant of the bargemen but soon to be their master. The next year an experiment was conducted on the section of the Forth and Clyde Canal, west of Lock 16 earlier used by Symington with small locomotive called the Victoria running along a single track pulling barges and passenger boats at respectable speeds. But again the Canal Company feared for the structure of their precious waterway and the experiment met the same fate as those of Symington.

Three years on and the railway age for Falkirk began in earnest. A passenger train carrying 1000 enthusiasts of the Glasgow and Edinburgh Railway reached Falkirk High Station, half a mile from the town, after a journey from Glasgow lasting one hour and a quarter.

> The sides of the railway were lined with admiring spectators, the bridge across the line, the station and every height which commanded a view of the train were crowded and young and old rent the air with their cheers.

The locomotive was fed with 'fresh water and coke', given a second engine and cheered on its way into the mouth of Falkirk's second long tunnel. Shortly thereafter four trains per day left the station to each of the great cities—first-class fares were four shillings and sixpence and third class, just half as much. The public had been admitted at a price to the new tunnel before the service commenced. The rough and ready track named from its function as the Cow Loan, re-named for the same reason as Coal Heugh Brae now became in part at least the High Station Road and passengers were collected by horse buses for the bumpy journey to the town centre.

In 1846 yet another line from Polmont to Stirling was routed through Falkirk by the Stirlingshire Midland Railway and a new station at Grahamston was constructed. The celebrated Skew Bridge at Laurieston was built to carry the line across the Edinburgh Road but the main road north from Falkirk to Carron had only a narrow footbridge for passengers with the horses and their heavy loads re-directed round the arc of McFarlane Crescent to rejoin the road fifty yards further on. Unsatisfactory as this was, it was not replaced by a proper stone bridge for another fifty years. The railway era heralded by these developments brought intense rivalry between two Companies which came to dominate the Scottish scene. The North British Railways Company took over the Edinburgh and Glasgow Company in 1865 and with it the Union Canal while the Caledonian Company acquired the Forth and Clyde Canal just two years later. With the North British taking control of the Grahamston line and the Caledonian running between Glasgow and Larbert, the battle for the lion's share of passenger and freight traffic in central Scotland was joined with a vengeance. This led inevitably to wasteful duplication of facilities but the scramble to extend rail services brought lines into every corner of the district. Soon new and expanding firms sought out sites near the track and great sidings and marshalling yards were built in the industrial heart of the town.

While the energies of many of Scotland's most prominent men of affairs were directed towards the great canal and the railways, Carron Company continued to prosper. Relations with the Canal Company were strained and for some years the partners were refused permission to make a special cut from the River Carron to the canal at Dalderse. This was eventually completed sometime before 1775 and greatly improved Carron's access to the sea until the course of the river itself was straightened a decade or so later. But there were a number of other problems. Gascoigne had left for Russia in 1786 with most of the firm's designs, a good deal of their special gun metal and many skilled workmen. Unfortunately for Carron he decided to stay there and set up an iron foundry for the Czar but the directors quickly overcame the loss by appointing Joseph Stainton as Manager in Gascoigne's place. He was soon a shareholder and able to promote the interests of other members of his family incuding his nephews Joseph and William Dawson.

Between them the Staintons and Dawsons ran Carron for nearly a hundred years and their canny and intelligent management of affairs ensured Carron's continued prosperity despite a rapid increase in competion from other foundries. The first of these to be formed in the district was the Dalderse Foundry Company established by George Sherriff on the north bank of the canal at Abbotshaugh in 1804. Sherriff had worked at Carron and with Boulton and Watt in Birmingham and he judged the markets strong enough to support a second producer in the district. He met with only moderate success and the firm closed its doors just six years later. In the same year a more determined bid to compete with the giant was launched by a group of gentlemen who recruited skilled men from Carron to form the Falkirk Foundry Company with premises on the Falkirk side of the canal next to the main road. As Falkirk Iron Company in the decades ahead it would spearhead the development of the Falkirk district as the nation's greatest centre for light castings and profoundly influence the lives of every bairn born in Falkirk for the next hundred years.

CHAPTER 7

Stentmasters and Feuars

During the second half of the 18th Century when Carron Company and the Great Canal were reshaping Falkirk's industrial and commercial future, the town's municipal affairs were in the doldrums. The ending of Livingston power after the first Jacobite defeat and the trauma of Prince Charlie's rising in 1745 had left Falkirk in disarray. It seems that the power to appoint baillies was retained by the Earl of Errol who occupied Callendar House until the purchase of the estates by William Forbes. But this was done infrequently and the baillies' powers were extremely limited. Eventually such appointments ceased. Control of affairs fell by default to a group of people who emerged sometime during the 17th Century as custodians of the burgh's water supplies. These Stentmasters as they were called, represented the merchants and craftsmen of the town and were elected by their fellows with four merchants and two each of the ten trades—masons, wrights and hammermen, weavers, tailors and shoemakers, brewers, fleshers, bakers and whipmen. In addition the four quarters of the town— Eastburn Bridge, Westburn Bridge, Vicar's Loan, and the Randy gate' as Kerse Lane was then called, were each allowed one member. These twenty-eight men met from time to time to 'cast the stent', that is, to fix an assessment which they expected the inhabitants of the burgh to pay towards the common services—especially water—provided in the town. There was no legal authority to back their decisions and only immemorial usage or 'use and wont' provided a justification for their activities. An estimate was made of an individuals' ability to pay and a stint of a pound or two set. The officer of the committee tried to collect what he could—his own wages depended on his success—but there was no attempt at enforcement beyond cultivating the notion of municipal pride and shared responsibility. Neither seem to have cut much ice with the canny bairns and the kitty was seldom full. In the 1720s, for example, the Kirk Session was approached by James Bowie described as a baillie in Falkirk and Richard Muirhead the clerk who wanted to borrow £20 for two months 'to meet the claim of the plumber for laying the pipes because they were unwilling to be hard upon the residents of the town untill the harvest be over.' The loan was granted!

Very occasionally a special effort was called for, though the result was often the same. In the early 1800s the wooden pipes of the original water supply were in such a poor condition that the Stentmasters decided to replace them with cast iron and to build a substantial cistern near the town centre. A piece of the garden ground behind the tenement lands on the south side of the High Street near the market place was obtained and in 1805 a wooden cistern was erected to hold 13,000 gallons of water drawn from the coal workings a mile to the south. After twenty years it was so decayed that Stentmasters were forced to replace it with a more substantial structure of stone and iron which remained in use until 1895 when it was converted into a public convenience. The street in which it stood was known as Cistern Lane until well into this century.

But the most celebrated venture of the Stentmasters was the erection of a new town steeple in 1814. Falkirk had, from the late 16th century at least, been a town with a tolbooth steeple. The first was replaced in 1697 by a building which adjoined the court and prison close to the present site in the High Street. In 1776 a clock was installed. In 1801 Forbes of Callendar allowed one William Glen to use the cellars of the Steeple and other buildings on condition that he did nothing to disturb the foundations. He did! Soon after, the steeple listed 15 inches eastwards; deemed dangerous it was 'cast to the ground' and the Stentmasters valiantly set about raising the necessary funds to replace it.

After a long legal wrangle with Glen they commissioned the celebrated architect David Hamilton, later the designer of Larbert Church, to produce proposals for a new steeple with clock, bell and prison rooms to house 'strolling vagrants and people who commit petty crimes'. The appeal for funds went to 'landed properties, merchants, farmers' who it was assumed, would want to 'subscribe liberally to such a laudable and useful undertaking'! The target was nearly £1,500 and predictably, less than a third of this was subscribed! Nonetheless, local builder Henry Taylor undertook the construction work and by June 1814 the 146 foot steeple was

The cross of Falkirk around 1820 from a contemporary engraving.

completed. The town's self appointed managers fell further into debt but despite this they celebrated their acquisition with the greatest possible gusto. Their new steeple certainly distinguished the town and was much admired by the many visitors—one hundred and eighty years later it still is!

In 1829 a group of business men in the town combined to form the Falkirk Gas Company with the intention of supplying private subscribers in the centre of the town. Nearly £1,700 was required to erect a gas works at East Bridge Street but it was operational by January the following year. The Stentmasters ever anxious to spend money they did not have, immediately set about trying to raise enough to erect gas lights in the same area. As usual they were only partially successful but nonetheless fifty-six lamps were eventually provided. Keeping them lit remained a costly business and for most of the summer, and on moonlit nights the lamplighter stayed at home! Despite this prudence the debts of the Stentmasters continued to grow just at the time when real central power in the town was most needed.

The steady growth of the town's population in the early decades of the 19th century, the total lack of central control of industrial

A view of Falkirk around 1820 from the south showing the new steeple, the new Parish Church and octagonal Tattie Kirk.

development and building, and the lack of such basic services as sewerage, adequate water supply or street paving or lighting, placed burdens on the Stentmasters which they were incapable of handling. Their influence waned and the state of the town declined alarmingly. But by the time the Stentmasters had launched their appeal for funds to replace the steeple, a powerful new group had emerged in Falkirk to challenge their position as sole municipal authorities.

In 1807 William Forbes of Callendar continuing his policy of enclosing grazing land and bringing it under cultivation turned his attention to the 150 acres of land to the south of the town which had been the common muir of Falkirk since the medieval period. The rights to graze stock, gather 'feal and divot' and quarry stones on this land was originally held by the fifteen inhabitants of the burgh who had obtained feus of land on which the old town was built. By a process known as subinfeudation the fifteen had by 1800 multiplied to over 200 and each of these Feuars as they came to be known could claim some part of the rights which were once the entitlement of the first fifteen. As Forbes' application to the Court of Session proceeded an offer emerged which formed the basis of the final settlement. He would enclose 120 acres for his own use and 20 for the use of the Feuars. The balance of 10 acres would be kept as common land for the Feuars' use much as before. In addition the Feuars would have one acre of land in Falkirk town centre where from 1801 the Horsemarket had been held, now Callendar Riggs, as well as the small customs or charges on grain and stock sold at the town markets. According to the legal decreet all of the income generated from land and customs had to be used for the benefit of the town or the Feuars, a distinction which would cause many difficulties over the succeeding decades. At first the Feuars were content to let the Stentmasters collect the rental raised on their land and the customs but within a few years, possibly fearing for the safety of their assets, they established a small committee to administer their own affairs. It was the start of a long period of strained relations between the two bodies which varied from close cooperation to open hostility and back again and was not resolved for fifty years.

At first the Feuars committee did little with the small sums raised by the customs and land except making the occasional donation to special causes, including it must be said, the Stentmaster's gas lamps. But the farmers of the carse whose crops were displayed on open tables at the weekly markets in the High Street began to complain about paying charges for no obvious benefit. A proposal to buy and sell outside the Regality boundary spurred the Feuars to action and in the late 1820s the search for a market site began. As usual there were great arguments and disputes before the small piece of land known as Dr Corbert's garden on the north side of the Parish Church was offered to the Feuars by two of their own number. On this site the 'new market' of Falkirk was erected consisting at first of fifteen 'shades' or sheltered areas for grain display and sale, later supplemented by a small granary of brick and wood. The ancient pathway across the glebe of the Kirk now formed the south boundary of the new market area—that is the present Newmarket Street. Though this proved far from satisfactory it secured the customs income for the Feuars for the time being and it certainly seemed to attract new business—in 1807 the duties had been only £22 but by 1851 they were over £100 per annum. By 1847 one observer was clearly impressed by the scale of activity:

> This days market is the second I have witnessed since it was held in its present place at the back of the Parish Church. I counted sixty five horses and carts all laden with grain standing in a row along the Glebe dyke, the backs of each cart to the footpath and the horses heads all in a line. They reached from the Minister's barn on to the gate of Aitken's Brewery. I never saw such a sight in Falkirk before.

But by the time the new market was open for regular business in 1830 the municipal arrangements such as they were had been given yet another shake up. In 1832 the great Reform Bill passed through Parliament and the following year the Scottish measure saw Falkirk, including the villages of Grahamston and Bainsford erected into a Parliamentary Burgh sharing a Member of Parliament with Lanark, Hamilton, Linlithgow and Airdrie. In the same year a new municipal constitution came into force which allowed for the election of a provost, three bailies and eight councillors but gave them only the most limited powers to raise money by assessing the property holders of the burgh. This amounted to a maximum of three pence in the pound, a trifling sum which could do no more than pay for the expenses of the administration. Even their modest judicial role was diminished the following year by the appointment of a Sheriff Substitute for the Eastern District of Stirlingshire, resident in

Falkirk and presiding in a Court House in the town. The frustration which was no doubt felt by successive administrations increased as the needs of the town strained the resources of the penniless Stentmasters and the canny Feuars. Falkirk was in a mess—three sets of managers without money or power and a steadily deteriorating fabric, failing water supply, inadequate lighting, unmade streets and an unhealthy population unable to resist the ravages of cholera which visited the town in the 1830s and 40s, and other killer illnesses that found a warm welcome in contaminated water supplies and overcrowded, insanitary hovels.

The turning point for the community was the publication in 1845 of Falkirk's first newspaper the 'Herald' which quickly began to draw attention to the short-comings of the town and asked questions of the so called managers. Who organised the Feuars? Was their money being used for the good of the community? Why did other towns adopt special measures to improve their facilities and not Falkirk? Stung by the criticism the Feuars embarked on a programme of major improvements between 1851 and 1859. The most significant was the causewaying of the High Street which was laid with granite blocks, and given pavements and a covered drain to carry away surface water. Over £1,000 of the Feuars funds went into this project along with subscriptions from gentlemen in the town especially those with houses or business premises in the street. The Feuars also contributed nearly £300 to assist the Stentmasters in maintaining the gas lamps in the burgh and over £100 to help search out new water supplies. But their biggest expenditure was to come. The continued increase in grain brought to their market led to renewed demands for better facilities. The Feuars conscious of the pressure they were under from their critics on the Council and in the local newspaper, made a bold and expensive move. In 1858 the shades were removed and a substantial new Corn Exchange was built to the design of Alexander Black of Falkirk. The Feuars borrowed around £1,500 to fund the new building in what might be seen as a desperate attempt to convince the people of the district that they had the good of the community at heart!

Pressure was certainly mounting to bring about fundamental change. Between 1848 and 1852 three attempts were made to convince the electors to support the adoption of a General Police Bill which would have given necessary finance raising powers but these were rejected. By 1858 a new administration under Provost

Thomas Keir was ready to try again, this time with a Bill tailor-made for Falkirk's special circumstances. It was introduced into Parliament the following year as 'An Act for Improving, Paving, Draining and Lighting the Burgh of Falkirk and for Regulating the Supply of Water within the Burgh; and for Providing for the Transference of the Property of the Stentmasters and Feuars of Falkirk to the Magistrates and Council.' On the face of it, the aims seem so obviously desirable that a quick passage of the Bill should have been the outcome. Nothing could have been further from the truth. In 1859 the simmering hostility between Feuars and Stentmasters erupted into open warfare, and the battle was fought not in a room in Wilson's Buildings or Rankines Folly but in the Committee rooms of the Houses of Lords and Commons in London. It was a poor advert for the spirit of cooperation of a Scottish town but a goldmine for the historian of the burgh for in page after page of charge and counter charge, the leading men of Falkirk described their town, with all its defects and defficiencies, in the minutest detail.

Foremost among the proposers of the Bill were Provost Keir and Robert Henderson, solicitor and clerk to the Stentmasters. They described the iniquities of the arrangements with three bodies managing affairs with no real power. But it was the general sanitary condition of the town which gave them greatest concern. Everywhere in the town, on the High Street and in the back closes and wynds were accumulations of filth, human and animal refuse and mud. Lack of drainage left 'large quantities of stagnant water, green in colour and offensive to the smell' especially in Grahamston and Bainsford but also in many parts of the old town. A water supply of around 3 gallons per day per person was only a quarter of what was required and it had to be carried from the public wells. It was too hard for washing purposes but could be drunk though 'sometimes it comes to the town the colour of porter or nearly so and it takes several hours for the mud to subside'. Robert Henderson complained that 'at times the scarcity has been so great that the water of the Union Canal has been used for domestic and culinary purposes. Water is in summer occasionally sold from barrels brought into the town.' With 'vegetable growth' in some of the pipes and 'frogs found in the wells' it was obvious that the health of the people was at considerable risk.

Lighting too was totally inadequate. The 56 gaslamps in Falkirk were less than half of the number required. There were 12 private lamps in the Main Street in Grahamston but none at all in Bainsford which was lit by the constant glare from the flashing blast furnaces of Carron half a mile further north. And these dark and dirty streets were the haunt of 'thieves and vagrants' from Edinburgh and Glasgow along with 'thimblers and cardplayers' who cheated the Falkirk 'bairns' out of their hard earned pennies. Another witness was the Procurator Fiscal, John Gair, who claimed that his own office in the High Street had been broken into three times recently and that most houses and business premises were the regular target for burglars. There were by 1857 a Superintendent, Sergeant and three police constables based in Falkirk but they were responsible for an area much greater than the Parliamentary Burgh and were still answerable to the Commissioners based in Stirling. There was no night watch in the town.

Perhaps the most telling evidence of all came from Mr James Girdwood a surgeon with a large practice in Grahamston and Falkirk and Rev Lewis Hay Irving, Minister of Falkirk Free Church and Chairman of the Sanitary Committee of the Parochial Board and one of the town's most influential citizens. Both were enthusiastic in their support for the Bill and scathing in their criticism of the town managers who allowed such deplorable conditions to continue. Mr Girdwood argued that the foul emissions from uncovered and blocked drains were responsible for high mortality in certain particular black spots. Many houses without any kind of toilet facilities were so filthy that many died of fever, croup and cholera. Mr Irving also claimed that many of the working people lived in buildings which were not fit for human occupation—he particularly highlighted a drain on the south boundary of the graveyard next to the back walls of High Street houses. Surface water drained through the lairs of the Kirkyard into this open sewer which was many feet about the level of the houses. All manner of foul and poisonous substances then found their way to the homes of the people in the very heart of the town. Typhoid fever was often the result. Fifty yards away on the junction of Wooer Street and the Back Row in one common lodging house it had claimed the lives of fifty people just a few years before. All the witnesses were clear as to the cause of the scandalous condition of their town, and all agreed on the solution. A single group of councillors with power to levy substantial assessments on the property owners of the whole burgh would raise the large sums needed to pave and drain and light the whole Parliamentary Burgh and provide an adequate and dependable supply of good water.

They presented a powerful and persuasive case but did not have it their own way by any manner of means. The opposition was formidable. The Feuars, mustered many of Falkirk's most influential figures and the picture they painted for the Lords and Members of the Commons was very different. Damning their opponents for gross exaggeration they claimed, quite rightly, that the public of Falkirk including the vast majority of the few hundred qualified electors were opposed to the Bill and especially the extra burdens it would place upon them. It was a 'most unnecessary and uncalled for Bill' said lawyer Adam Smith because 'Falkirk is so well governed already'. Auctioneer James Neilson was outspoken in his defence of the Feuars record and of the town whose 'Main Street is the cleanest street I ever saw in my life'. Former Provost, Robert Adam himself a Feuar and one-time supporter of such reforms was incensed by the attempt to take away the Feuars property and rights and use it for people 'outside the blue line', that is, beyond the old Regality boundary in Grahamston and Bainsford. From the other side of the line, Bainsford blacksmith William Drummond took a different perspective. The people of Bainsford didn't want the Stentmasters' debts (or the Feuars' for that matter although he did not say so!)—nor did the village need drainage, water supply or causewaying. The shocked Advocate for the proposers suggested that Bainsford sounded like 'a garden of Eden', which Drummond did not dispute! As far as lighting was concerned, Carron's flames were a blessing.

> The darker the night, the greater the illumination .... at all times of dark nights it is illuminated so much so that I believe a Gas burner would be like the Moon when the sun is shining!

A second medical man, Dr David Hadden, disputed the claims of surgeon Girwood. He too regularly visited throughout the district and found the people to be healthy and the state of the town not injurious to their wellbeing. Statistics were produced to show that the town's mortality rate a year or so before had been less than that of Stirling, Airdrie, Lanark and Campsie and well below the overall Scottish figure. All in all it was an uncompromising and determined opposition summed up by Adam Smith 'I would not' he said, 'be disposed to entrust such powers to a Municipal body, but with respect to a Community like Falkirk it would be perfect madness'.

Madness or no, it came to pass, for the Bill was approved in August 1859, the Feuars retained their Corn Exchange and land but lost the power to collect customs. The Stentmasters property, steeple and water pipes and wells, and their debts passed into the hands of 'Commissioners' as the municipal councillors were to be called for a period. Perhaps the obvious sincerity of Dr Girdwood and Rev. Irving had carried the day against a group so obviously out to protect vested interests and prevent a fair sharing of the burdens. A telling remark by Adam Smith underlined the prevailing attitude and perhaps helped to sway any doubters who remained. Asked if he would approve even a three-farthing increase in the rates to improve the High Street, he replied:

> If the town were my own and I wished to give it all the amenities of a private house fitted for a genteel family I would .... but with reference to the Inhabitants, I think the three-farthings is too much.

The Parliament decided that men like Smith should no longer manage the affairs of the 'inhabitants' and put their trust in those whose aims were more in tune with the times. It would be difficult to exaggerate the importance of the Bill in changing the course of Falkirk's history. If the charter of James VI in 1600 was the birth certificate of the burgh then 1859 was its coming of age. After a long and painful adolescence the new burgh was set fair for a period of unrivalled prosperity.

CHAPTER 8

Church and School in Victorian Falkirk

In the early 18th Century, at the same time as the Livingston's baronial control was extinguished in the district, the power of the one remaining authority, the church, was diminished by division and secession. The promise of freedom for sessions and presbyteries which the settlement of 1688 had offered had been dashed in 1712. The Patronage Act of that year more or less restored the power of landowners to impose ministers of their choice even when sessions and church members disagreed. Several serious disputes arose but the first major challenge came in 1733 when Ebenezer Erskine of Stirling and three other ministers formed an Associate Presbytery independent of the Church of Scotland. Seven elders of Falkirk Parish asked for the supply of a minister and in 1742 they acquired 'all and whole, that big yard lying on the north side of

The Silver Row building of the original Erkine Church which later housed the Roxy Theatre. The Friendly Hotel and parts of Callendar Square stand on the site today.

the town near the east', that is on the high ground between High Street and Manor Street on what was Silver Row. A plain 'meeting house' with accommodation for 950 'sitters' was erected and became the second church of the town. The whole area has been transformed by modern development though the Friendly Hotel stands close to the site of the first Erskine building. Of course the new session claimed all the power of the old with the rights and duties that went with it. This included of course bringing the sabbath breakers and the rest to public repentence, with this time one added serious offence—attending services at the established church! Such a split obviously reduced the absolute authority claimed by the Minister and elders of the Parish Church,—it was easy now to dismiss a call to 'compear' by claiming adherence to the opposition!

The power of the established church in Falkirk, thus diminished was further reduced forty years later by a second secession. This time a small group of ministers led by Thomas Gillespie in Dunfermline, established a new Presbyterian church free from the oppression of state or any other interference. He found support in Falkirk and in 1767 a Relief congregation was established in the town. Thirty years later they had their own permanent place of worship at the west end, later known as the West Church. This building served a variety of Presbyterian groups for two centuries until 1991 when it became the Falkirk home of the People's Church, a lively and growing evangelical congregation. It remains the oldest public building in Falkirk and local historians as well as the people of the town must be delighted to see it continue serving the community in the way its founding fathers had intended.

The departure of still more of its active members dealt the Parish Church another blow at a time when it had difficulties enough to contend with. The old Kirk building was wearing badly. Some repair work had been done and a new steeple added in 1735, but it was, what it was, a three hundred year old building, cold and dark, damp and cramped, built for a style of worship no longer appropriate and incapable of accommodating the congregation it was meant to serve. A new age demanded new and better facilities. The money to provide improvement was available and it required only a catalyst to spark the Session and the reluctant landowners into action. In 1794 a new minister was called, Dr. James Wilson and the difficult task fell to him.

From his arrival in Falkirk until his death 35 years later, he was an energetic and controversial figure provoking hostility and opposition from large numbers of his congregation and affection and regard from as many others. He quickly settled to what seemed to him, the principal task facing the parish—the replacement of the old inadequate church which by the 1790s looked beyond repair. The new minister was quite clear in his own mind that the crumbling edifice had to go and he set about convincing the principal landowners of the Parish whose responsibility it was, of the need for a new church. At first he was reasonably successful and most of these 'heritors' including Lord Dundas agreed to the proposal. In 1797 he was in confident mood as he wrote the Falkirk entry for the famous Statistical Account of Scotland.

> The building is..... far from being sufficient for the accommodation of those who wish to attend; but it is hoped something will soon be done to provide a remedy for this inconvenience.

But he had forgotten the formidable William Forbes of Callendar who had other ideas and was, like Wilson himself, not easily diverted from his own particular path. At his insistence surveyors were asked to report on the possibilities of repairing the church and while they did agree that it could be done they were doubtful if any extension was possible without great additional expense. The debate dragged on and the years passed. Forbes changed his line. He would agree to the rebuilding of the church on a new site selected by him—he offered the corner of Hope Street and New Market Street where the Sheriff Court now stands. Wilson and his Session were firm in their resistance—the ground of the old Kirk was hallowed by centuries of worship and it would not be abandonded lightly. Eventually the dispute reached the Court of Session and from the welter of charge and countercharge a compromise solution emerged far nearer the wish of the Minister than that of his principal parishioner. The tower of the old church would remain and all the rest would come down—a new building designed by Gillespie Graham of Edinburgh of oblong shape lying east to west abutting the tower on the north side would be built to accommodate a congregation of over 800 seated in semi-circular form facing in towards the pulpit in the centre of the new north wall. In 1810 work commenced and the present church began to

The Parish Church built in 1811. The square tower which was retained from the pre Reformation building shows the gable marks of the old south aisle where the Livingstons were buried.

take shape. By the following August it was ready for occupation and the heritors met to share out the seating in proportion to the value of their property holding in the parish. Not surprisingly then that first seating plan, which survives, is dominated by Forbes of Callendar and Lord Dundas who have the use of most of the places for themselves, their families and the more fortunate of their tenants. The early estimates had costed the new building at £3,593 2s 6d but in the event over £5,000 was expended before that great day when we are told that the new Kirk was opened.

> with due solemnity upon Sabbath, the eighth day of September, one thousand eight hundred and eleven years amid a great concourse of people.

Dr Wilson's drive and determination had secured the new building but his moderate approach to discipline particularly did not please all his congregation. The grip of the church on the people was

The Tattie Kirk, an unusual octagonal building which housed the Antiburgher congregation from 1806 to 1879 and still survives as a showroom and store.

slipping and more and more of the new industrial workers found themselves with neither church nor minister near enough or concerned enough to serve their needs. Those who pined for the tough old days of stern unbending pastors found their way to the breakaway groups though once the habit of splintering is estab-lished it is difficult to stop. The original Erskine group divided and divided again so that by the early years of the 19th Century there were congregations in the original Horsemarket Lane Church, an antiburgher group in the curious little octagonal building in the Cow Wynd known to later generations as the 'Tattie Kirk,' and still another in a building in Cistern Lane behind the High Street tenements. All claimed to be the real Church of Scotland, true to the reforming fathers vision and all claimed power to assist the poor, and maintain discipline. Along with the Relief Church and the Parish Church that gave Falkirk five separate congregations but for the divided establishment much worse was to come.

The 1830s were a time of growing difficulty for the national church with more and more ministers and lay members joining the chorus of protest over what they saw as the State's interference in spiritual affairs. This dispute once again turned on the vexed question of lay patronage, that is, on who had the right to nominate a new minister for a vacant charge. But there was more to the growing polarisation among fathers and brethren than mere questions of interference and spiritual freedom—it was a struggle for the very soul of the church itself with the protest led for the most part by the evangelicals and rejected by more moderate elements. By 1840 it seemed that a breach was inevitable and their new minister William Begg warned his Falkirk congregation that many ministers would have to 'give up their livings for conscience sake'. He strongly supported the protest and seemed set to join the objectors when the great Disruption finally came. But the period was a complex one with many different standards of opinion woven and twisted into a tangle which no short summary can unpick. Suffice to say that for some ministers a middle way emerged which meant they could sustain their protest yet remain within the establishment. Begg was one of them and though his friends were greatly disappointed at his decision, it is a considerable tribute to his personal integrity and standing in the community that he retained their friendship and regard. Indeed when that great break came at last in May 1843 and thousands of ministers, elders and lay members abandoned their churches to support the new Free Church, relations in Falkirk remained reasonably close unlike many other areas where acrimonious dispute further scarred an already damaged Presbyterian reputation.

The day before the final disruption took place, a meeting was held in the Baptist Chapel in Bank Street at which two Falkirk elders John Burns and Thomas Hardie took the platform—many people attended and pledged themselves to follow the leadership into the new Free Church. How many did so is uncertain though we do have recorded a telling remark from one elder who remained within the established church who told a leading free churchman in the town that 'your numbers are not great but you have the cream of the congregation with you'. This new congregation met first in the church in Cistern Lane moving eventually to Garrison Place and finally to New Market Street in 1896, the present St Andrews Church.

In the same year as this great disruption shook the church to its very foundations an event took place almost unnoticed which was in its way as revolutionary and far reaching in its effect on the religious life of the district. In May, Father Paul MacLachlan from Glenlivet officiated at the opening ceremony of the first Roman Catholic Church in the district for nearly three centuries. The Catholic religion had been all but extinguished in the years after the Reformation but the great public works, the roads, canals, and railways brought large numbers of immigrant workers from Ireland and the Highlands for whom there was no place of worship or ministering priest. Father MacLachlan who was responsible for the whole of Stirlingshire began visiting the town in 1831 and occasionally held services in private houses and public buildings like the Assembly Rooms in the Pleasance or in the Railway Hotel on the High Station Road. By 1840 there were 180 in his congregation which was meeting weekly and the new church in Hope Street dedicated to the missionary St Francis Xavier was the culmination of years of struggle. Designed by the architect William Stirling of Dunblane, it was described as 'an elegant structure in the Saxon style which forms a conspicuous object in the thriving town of Falkirk'. The building which had seating for 600 and had to serve a huge area of east Stirlingshire, was lost following a fire in 1955 and replaced by the present modern building in 1961.

Many other reformed churches outside the Presbyterian fold were established from time to time. Some flourished briefly, declined and closed down, but others were more persistent and their descendents remained active until well into this century. A host of public buildings were pressed into service to accommodate new congregations—a hall in Swords Wynd off the High Street housed an early Baptist group while congregationalists met in what later became the Bank Street premises of Young's Stores. In the same street the Evangelical Union finally settled in a new building, later St. Modans Church and now the lower storey of the Bank Street Bingo Hall!

The Episcopalian tradition which had suffered in the final settlement of the religious question in 1688 had survived in the hearts and homes of some of the gentry but it was probably the arrival of a large contingent of skilled English workers and their families which led to the revival of services in the area. Certainly there are records of fortnightly meetings in Carron in the 1790s and visits by the Earl of Dunmore's chaplains to Wilson's Buildings and other halls during the following century. In 1863 a fine new church was built in Kerse Lane to the design of the celebrated Edinburgh architect Sir Robert Rowand Anderson then at the start of an illustrious career. Financed in large measure by Forbes of Callendar and other leading landowners it remains one of the most beautiful buildings in the whole Falkirk district.

Badly buffeted by winds of division and opposition the Parish Church nonetheless held on and began to grow once more. The rapid increase in population brought repeated demands from the outlying areas of the burgh and the villages of the parish for a church and minister of their own. It was a remarkably complex legal and financial matter to achieve this laudable aim and most had to wait long years and suffer great neglect before their wish was granted. Camelon Parish was the first in 1853, though there had been a church there since 1840. Later still came Grahamston, Bonnybridge and Grangemouth.

As we have seen, the role of the church in society had changed steadily over the years as fragmentation reduced personal adherence to one particular congregation. Discipline of the kind familiar to earlier bairns disappeared and cutty stools and pillars faded into memory. A gentler message offered in more pleasant surroundings was the way of the new age, still harsher than our own era perhaps but nonetheless a transformation for all that. Stained glass windows, delicate architectural details, carved wooden pews, harmoniums and organs, gas mantles and warm welcoming Carron stoves appeared throughout the town as congregations, wealthy from the flourishing iron foundries and fertile lands of the carse, erected handsome new premises.

The plain Relief Kirk at the west end was given a fine new entrance in 1883, the old Tattie Kirk was abandoned in 1879 and a new building (demolished in 1990) built in Graham's Road. And so it went on—a new Congregational Church in Meeks Road opened in 1893, a handsome Methodist Chapel in James Street in 1892 and a Baptist Church in Orchard Street in 1897. It is plain that the church, taken as a whole, was continuing to play a very significant part in the life of the population despite more than a century of division, but its traditional role in affairs was certainly changing.

By the middle of the century poor relief, once the exclusive province of the Kirk Sessions had more or less passed into the hands of other agencies and in 1872 parish schools were detached from the control of the church and handed over to new School

Boards. But the new bodies still relied heavily on the energy and expertise of ministers of the town churches. Lewis Hay Irving of the Free Church has already been encountered in his role as proponent of the Bill to change the deplorable state of the town— like William Begg of the Parish Church and James Aitchison of the Erskine, Irving was involved in a very wide range of activities, helping to establish schools for poor children, building asylums for the very old and insane and encouraging further beneficial public works. These Ministers along with the powerful and wealthy men on their Sessions remained the leading figures in burgh affairs in an era when the growing division between the haves and have nots plagued the industrial areas of prosperous Victorian Scotland.

They and their earnest congregations did what they thought best though it seems pitifully little with hindsight—each Monday from the first week of November for example, ladies of the Dorcas Society gathered to make clothes for the needy to ease the special problems of winter. In January 1884 for example, they distributed '25 petticoats, 4 shifts, 13 dresses for the women and girls, 5 pairs of boots, 6 shawls and turnovers, 14 boys shirts and 5 semits'. A few years earlier the Falkirk Session had noted that '88 people in the town had each received 3/6d'

But despite the best intentions of ministers and congregations, despite new Church buildings galore and more active communicant members than ever, the church as a whole was slowly losing the battle. The growing urban population, many living in wretched poverty, were finding their solace in other ways and Falkirk, regardless of its fine new fabric, was increasingly the scene of drunkenness and violence and what a later age would call multiple deprivation.

We have already encountered the parochial schoolmasters of Falkirk in the century after the Reformation struggling to fulfil the lofty vision of the founding fathers against the indifference of the majority of the heritors of the parish. These leading landowners were legally obliged to fund a school house and a master but most often they sought to provide the bare minimum demanded by the law and sometimes even less. In the early 18th Century we find the school in a slightly better situation. Moving from the Kerse Lane to 'my Lord Callendar's lodging' near the junction of Vicar's Loan and the Back Row. Here in the old town house of the ancient family it remained for fifty years with a succession of masters offering a diet of reading, writing, arithmetic and religious education, with the more able children going on to study Latin and sometimes Greek. Although the term 'Grammar School' of Falkirk appears first in 1712, it was many decades before the two streams—the elementary 'parish school' and the more advanced 'grammar school' were clearly identified. In 1761 the Session agreed to rehouse the school in the unused nave of the church to the west of the tower. This was twenty five feet long and for the princely sum of £20 the elders refurbished the building and created two classrooms. But with demand for places at the school continuing to grow the heritors were forced just fourteen years later to provide a completely new building in the Back Row. It was this school which drew the praise of Rev James Wilson in his report for the Statistical Account in 1797. 'The grammar school of Falkirk' he said, 'is justly held in great reputation' and, in an aside which would no doubt find an echo in educational circles in every age, he concluded:

> Though populous and flourishing situations like Falkirk yield a decent competence for the support of respectable schoolmasters, yet in few situations are they paid in proportion to their usefulness in society.

There were already several adventure schools running successfully in the town, and the hostility which the Session had once shown, had given way to an acceptance that the official schools could not possibly cope with the demand from seven or eight hundred children.

By 1803 the Falkirk School was in a 'ruinous condition' but repairs kept it operating, though overcrowding continued to be a feature for another forty years. An additional building was acquired in the Pleasance with one large room for the teaching of English but just six years later the Master, Thomas Downie, petitioned the heritors, complaining about the size of his room and the inadequacy of the furnishings for the numbers attending—more than one hundred pupils in a room eighteen foot square! He claimed then that his health was threatened by this situation and it was possibly his early death five years later at the age of just thirty-nine that first prompted the heritors to look once again at the situation.

Certainly the new master, James Burns, was far from happy with his facilities. He pressed the heritors for action and in response they appointed an investigating committee which soon confirmed the schoolmasters opinion. They found both the parochial school in the Back Row and the English school in the Pleasance in 'a miserable state—damp, low-roofed, small in size and a very bad situation'. The English room which Downie had found so oppressive plus another large room close by, now contained over 200 children. In an astonishing account Burns described his day-to-day situation.

> of these 133 write in the following order:- 54 write on tables, 24 write on forms, kneeling on the floor: 45 stand, who have neither tables nor forms, but I endeavour to give them fifteen or twenty minutes by making them change places with some of those sitting at table or lying at forms. I have sufficient forms for 130 only and there are 72 who have no seats.

Despite this damning indictment the heritors continued to resist the demand for a new school though they did ask the magistrates of the burgh to assist then in solving the problem. The outcome was a decision in 1844 to build a new school in the town and after much wrangling a site to the north of the Back Row 'an out of the way, low and unwholesome place' according to one of the objectors, was acquired for the purpose. Two new streets were opened up linking the school to the rest of the town—Park Street running north from the Back Row and Weir Street running east from Vicars Loan. Despite the refusal of the Feuars to contribute to the cost,

The Grammar School of Falkirk in Park Street opened in 1846. It is still used for educational purposes. *Photograph* Michael Middleton

Silver Row viewed from the Callendar Riggs showing St Francis' Catholic School
built in 1880 to replace the original which was in Manor Street or the Back Row
as it was then called.

£1,500 was raised by the heritors and through voluntary donations,
and on May 18th 1846 the children marched in a procession from
the Pleasance to Park Street where many of the leading men of the
town joined them in celebration. The building remained as the
Grammar and Parochial School for more than fifty years and later
housed the County Mining Institute. Now as the town centre base
for the Community Education service it continues to serve the
educational needs of the people of the district.

From 1846 the Grammar and Parochial Schools flourished
under the guidance of a succession of outstanding masters. By 1860
the list of subjects available included French, German, Arithmetic,
Book-keeping, Mathematics, Writing, Drawing and Music as well as
English, Greek and Latin. From age six to ten children attended
the parish school with the most able remaining in the Grammar
School section. By the 1850s there were nearly 400 pupils in all and
a decade later an extension was required to alleviate serious overcrowding.

If the Parish School was the heart of Falkirk's educational system, it was very far from the only provision. As early as 1800 there were fourteen teachers in the parish with small schools in Camelon, Grangemouth, Bonnybridge and Laurieston supported by individuals or groups of business people in each location. Thereafter a number of highly successful and long lasting institutions emerged to serve the needs of particular groups. The Bainsford Self-Supporting School lasted from 1797 until it was absorbed into the Northern School eighty years later. At its height it offered elementary education to nearly 200 children. Half a mile away in Grahamston a Subscription School was established by the inhabitants in 1810 and it provided both day and evening education to children and to young bank clerks, apprentice merchants and surveyors, or seamen who came to learn the arts of mathematics and navigation. There was a Free Church school in Meeks Road from 1851 and a Catholic School in the Back Row from 1853, as well as many others—a Charity School supported by active church members, offered basic education to around 70 children of poor families. From 1813 onwards it offered Bible studies, reading and writing and so many people wished to support the work that a new school in Pleasance Square was built in 1851. Six years later another church initiative this time from Rev Lewis Hay Irving saw the establishment of a Ragged and Industrial School to provide for the orphans, waifs and strays of the district. By 1869 fifty boys were effectively in the custody of the Master in the school in the Kerse Lane, where bible study and basic education and useful work was the diet intended to reclaim these least favoured of all the bairns of the industrial burgh. Their building served this century as a model lodging house and was demolished in the summer of 1991.

But of all the educational initiatives in Victorian Falkirk the one that most seems to catch the popular sentiment of the age was the school run in Bryson Street, Bainsford for over fifty years from 1820 by James Grossart. He was the most celebrated teacher of his day though he had no formal qualifications. Grossart's school was a mecca for people of all ages seeking instruction in a bewildering variety of subjects. One former pupil remembered Grossart's classroom as a place of wonderment.

> Above the entrance door was a music board, which had always some new song or hymn on it, in staff or sol-fa notation. They saw the walls covered by maps mostly of his own painting. Above the fireplace were

illustrations of the principles of mechanics. At the south-west corner, over the slate press, was a working model of a steam-engine in sections, all made by his own hands. The centre ornament of the roof was the mariner's compass, with all the points carefully painted in true position. The remainder of the roof was covered with various constellations of the starry firmament. All of these were at hand for illustration in his teaching, and many others besides. He managed to keep a crowded school going in full swing, from the infants in one corner to the sailors in the other learning navigation, with no pupil-teachers, only a monitor appointed now and then to call out the names of bad boys, who got their reward at his convenience. Whoever heard Mr Grossart recite 'Mary, the Maid of the Inn,' and did not feel every hair standing up and their blood curdling? He seemed to throw his whole soul into it, and photographed the picture on their minds.

Grossart's combination of education for the sheer pleasure of learning with the development of practical skills of real value, seem the very embodiment of the intellectual spirit of the age and many of his pupils went on to play a leading role in the rapid expansion of the town's industry and commerce after the middle of the 19th Century.

But despite the excellence of such individual efforts the whole picture in the district as well as the country as a whole, was a patchwork of quality and insufficiency, high standards and deplorable inadequacy, depending on large measure on charity or the forced contribution of unwilling landowners. It was ripe for change and in 1873 following the Act of the previous year most of Falkirk eighteen schools were removed from the control of Sessions, private groups or individuals and placed under Parochial Boards elected by the ratepayers of the burgh. Most benefited greatly from the change, though there was great regret that under the particular terms of the Act the Grammar School was reduced to no more than one of many providing elementary education. For several years pupils capable of higher study were forced to travel to the cities but Rev James Aitchison, Minister of the United Presbyterian (Erskine) Church, campaigned tirelessly for a change of heart. In 1886 the Parochial Board agreed at last to designate the old Grammar School as a High School and soon over 350 pupils were in attendance. A decade later the old buildings proved inadequate and in 1889 a superb new school was opened in Rennie Street. It served as the Falkirk High for more than 60 years before that school moved to their present modern premises in 1962. The old buildings became Woodlands School in the same year.

Another new school provided by the Parochial Board was Comely Park opened in 1879 with over 300 children, most of whom had attended the Charity School in the Pleasance. Known by many as 'Cochranes Academy' after its first Headmaster, it was soon too small for the number of pupils and required to be extended early in the new century. In 1909 it had a role of over a thousand pupils.

In 1827 in common with many Scottish towns Falkirk saw the establishment of a Mechanics Institute under the name of the School of Arts. In one of the earliest statements of aims the founders proposed 'the instruction of mechanics and others in Popular Science and the Useful Arts—by means of lectures, apparatus, models and a library'. Meeting first in the versatile Assembly Rooms—rented for £2. 15 shillings, 'coal and candles not supplied'—the School soon had over 100 members and well known lecturers were engaged to give talks on various branches of physics, as well as astronomy, anatomy and zoology. By the 1830s it had moved on to the larger Independent Chapel in Bank Street and the lectures were attracting more than two hundred. Despite this there were always financial difficulties and for a period from 1844 the school ceased to function. When it reopened a few years later the trend away from scientific subjects towards literature, music, philosophy and history became even more marked and the School changed from an educational institution for artisans into a culture club for a more leisured class. By 1862 very large musical evenings were being held in the new Corn Exchange in Newmarket Street and this continued through to the Town Hall which replaced it around twenty years later. By then there were a number of other organisations particularly church groups offering 'soirees and conversatziones' with musical interludes as well as talks and lectures on all manner of subjects. In the face of this growing competition the School of Arts ceased to exist after 1891 but by then the town had a substantial building knows as the School of Arts and Sciences opposite the old Grammar School in Park Street. It was opened by Lord Roseberry in 1878 as a response no doubt to growing demands in the rapidly expanding iron industry for skilled designers and technically competent workmen. A few years after Park Street became the new High School the School of Arts and Science building became a department of the school. After a century of odd jobs in the education service including a spell as the school meals kitchen it is now the home of Falkirk College Art and Design section—a happy return indeed to its original purpose.

With fine new schools for children of all ages as well as adults, and the legal and financial framework to support the work of the teachers, Falkirk was at last freed from the piecemeal provision of the previous centuries. The reformers' dream of adequate education for every child in the Parish no matter their means was fulfilled at last. It had only taken three hundred years!

CHAPTER 9

Building a New Town

Despite the enormous impact of Carron ironworks and the steady growth of Falkirk Iron Company, Falkirk in the mid 19th Century was still primarily a market centre serving the landward area of East Stirlingshire and the villages of the carse. Population growth over the previous fifty years had been steady though not spectacular and was just under 9,000 by 1851. Describing the town around the same period, the Falkirk lawyer James Burns claimed that 'with the exception of leather, no goods are to any extent manufactured in the town'. But he listed the works which had grown up on the outskirts of the old burgh, especially along the line of the canal—a sawmill in Bainsford 'wrought by three steam engines' employing 15, two pyroligneous acid works in Grahamston making 'iron liquor for the print fields and vinegar', and a distillery at Rosebank. Forty-two men worked in the town's four tanneries and there were of course the collieries, woodyards, cornmills, brick and tile works and James Aitken's ale and porter brewery. But one in five of the workforce was already engaged in the iron industry and in the second half of the 19th century this increased dramatically as the population almost doubled to over 16,000. More than a dozen new foundries opened their doors as the national and international demand for domestic cast iron multiplied. In 1856 Abbots Foundry opened on the site of the short lived Dalderse Iron Works. This was followed by Burnbank in 1860, Cockburns in 1864, Grahamston close by in 1868 and Callendar in 1876. By 1900 these five were employing over 1000 men using iron from the Carron blast furnaces to produce an enormous range of goods from pots and pans, to stoves, grates, boilers, pipes and ranges. Outside the town the same thing was happening in Larbert, Denny, Bonnybridge, Camelon and Laurieston and there seemed no limit to the markets for their products. Many of the foundry employers built houses for the workforce and men were attracted to the town in large numbers by the prospect of steady employment no matter

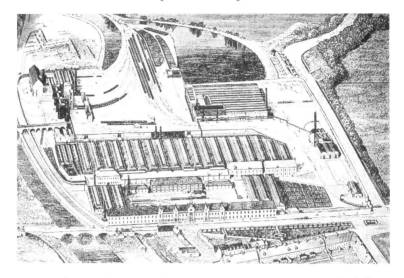

An aerial view of Carron Works in the 1880s showing the new layout including
the office block in the foreground and the canal from the works to the harbour

how punishing or unpleasant. In the face of the challenge, Carron
Company, itself enjoying a boom period, decided on a huge
programme of reconstruction. Under the leadership of David
Cowan, the works were completely re-built in the late 1870s with
new blast furnaces, foundries and brickworks and that splendid
office block which was the subject of much argument in recent
years. The battle to keep it standing while all other vestiges of the
great undertaking disappeared, was untimately in vain despite
Findlay Russell's valiant campaign. Only the central bay remains
but in such a horrendous setting that it has lost all the dignity and
style it once enjoyed.

At the end of the century four out of ten men in the burgh were
employed in the iron industry and east Stirlingshire was firmly
established as the nation's principal centre for light castings. It was
to remain so for another fifty years and for much of the time the
vast fortunes earned by the companies were retained by the families
who owned and managed them, and who invested substantial sums
in the religious and commercial life of the burgh.

Employment in agriculture and the manufacture of goods associated with the land declined markedly over the same period as the
old market town became a thriving new industrial centre. Two

James Aitken's Brewery new building opened in 1900. By then they had been brewing on the same site for well over 150 years.

firms which prospered from the growing band of thirsty ironworkers were James Aitken the brewers who by the early decades of the 19th Century were firmly established on the large site on the north side of Newmarket Street, and Robert Barr whose mineral water works were located on the other side of the High Street at Burnfoot. Aitken's Ales enjoyed tremendous popularity throughout Britain and as demand increased towards the end of the century, the brewery was completely reconstructed. The magnificent red brick building with its familiar high chimney came to dominate the skyline and the aroma which cloaked the town on brewing days was as much a part of Falkirk as the Steeple bell or the distant fire of the Carron furnaces. Barr's story began in 1830 when the first Robert Barr started a business cutting corks by hand on the site at Burnfoot. Among his customers were several aerated water manufacturers and when, fifty years later machine cut corks drove his son out of business, Robert Barr junior switched trades and a legend was born. By the end of the century the company had prospered to the extent that it had branches in Glasgow and Lanarkshire and was soon able to buy out many of its Falkirk competitors.

The rapid growth in Falkirk's population in the second half of the 19th century did not immediately produce an extension to the physical size of the town and, inevitably, overcrowding and further deterioration of the already inadequate housing was the result. At one time when power and wealth lay in the hands of a small number of landowners they lived in the landward area and kept town houses within the burgh. The rest, whatever their station, lived together in the crowded streets and wynds. But as the 19th Century progressed the new men of affairs, the lawyers and bank

The celebrated Glasgow Buildings in Williamson Street demolished in the 1960s.

agents, ironmasters and brewers began to acquire fine new houses outwith the old burgh limits. Old mansion houses like Thornhill, Kersehill, Arnotdale and Gartcows were rebuilt or restored, and many handsome new villas were constructed in Arnothill. Later, in the Meeks Road and Woodlands areas, north and south of the railway line through Grahamston, large numbers of villas and cottages were built for the traders and business people and in 1888 the Town Council erected lodging houses and 'artisans dwellings' for 200 at a cost of nearly £10,000. One of these blocks in Williamson Street was the famous 'Glasgow Buildings', a well known spot in Falkirk folk lore, which was demolished in the 1960s. This was the first example of municipal housing in the burgh and, commendable though it was, it left vast numbers in miserable conditions. The efforts of architects and masons were for the most part engaged in a quite different activity.

Within the burgh it was new public buildings which began to

The Sheriff Court building opened in 1868 at the west end of the town. The
police station on the left was added a few years later. The Gentleman Fountain
was removed in 1923.

appear from the mid century on, reflecting commercial success and
growing municipal pride and self confidence. The first of these was
the new Sheriff Court House on the corner of Newmarket and
Hope Streets. For many years from 1834 successive Sheriffs dis-
pensed justice in a variety of inadequate public halls like the
familiar Assembly Rooms, Wilson's Buildings, the Red Lion Inn in
the High Street and the Temperance Hotel, later Young's pram
store on the south side of Bank Street which was purchased in 1852
and converted into a proper court building. But plans for a more
permanent solution incorporating prison cells were already underway—by 1850 the familiar west end site had been acquired from
the Falkirk Brewery Company and despite long years of wrangling
between the Town Council and the Stirlingshire Commissioners,
the new building was finally ready in 1868. Designed by the Edinburgh architects, Brown and Peddie in the popular Scots baronial
style, it cost nearly £8,000 and served for over 120 years. It closed
in 1990 and the business was transferred to the superb new building in Camelon Main Street.

A decade after the new Court House opened for business the
Town Council, anxious to find a permanent home for its growing

The Town Hall in Newmarket Street opened in 1879 and demolished in the late 1960s.

band of officials, commissioned local architect William Black to design a building for the corner of New Market Street and Glebe Street. The result was the attractive baronial style building still known to most Falkirk folk as the 'Burgh Buildings' which served as the municipal centre for nearly a century. In 1975 it was scheduled for demolition as part of the re-development of the brewery site but a determined campaign led by that doughty fighter James Middlemass eventually succeeded in saving the building. It did more than that—it proved to the people that it was possible to resist the worst excesses of the planners if the will was strong enough. The unnecessary destruction has continued of course, but not with such ease or contempt for the views of the public. The building now serves the Social Work Department of Central Region and also contains the Registrar of Births, Deaths and Marriages.

In 1877 the Feuars of Falkirk bereft of much of their power but still influential in the affairs of the town, decided to replace the Corn Exchange. It was less than twenty years old but the demands placed upon it for public meetings and entertainment were steadily increasing and the building could not cope. It had been built as a grain market with some use for public purposes—now its replacement would reverse the scheme—a Town Hall for the burgh with some space set aside for the diminishing corn trade. Again the architect was William Black and the Town Hall and the new

Masonic Lodge of Falkirk next door were completed in 1879. The Feuars expressed the hope that their new hall would 'in generations to come, be looked upon as the home of music in our town and from which would proceed elevating and refining influences in this and the sister arts'. For almost a hundred years it was at the heart of the community, constantly thronged for political meetings and election results, choral and orchestral concerts, displays and demonstrations, school prize givings and church socials. Great public appeals were launched within its walls and many of the most famous performers in the land graced its stage. With the possible exception of the old Kirk and the Steeple, no building in Falkirk was so prized, but that did not save it from the bulldozers in 1966. With a new, modern building in West Bridge Street, the old Hall was surplus to requirements, or so it was said. Down it came and with it the back wall of the Parish Church! Further building on the site was deemed impossible without more permanent damage and plans to build a Church Hall were abandoned. The space stands empty today—a constant reminder to those who still recall the Town Hall with affection and regret. But all that was in the future.

In 1879 the Feuars may have thought that the investment would restore their power but only eleven years later the Falkirk Corporation Act was passed by Parliament which transferred all their properties to the Town Council. This of course included land which has remained in use as public property ever since, the 30 acres on which Lochgreen Hospital and Princes Park were later sited, the Blinkbonny or 'Low' Park and Poors House and the 'Washing Green' on High Station Road, which later housed the burgh stables then the electricity power station. In the town centre the one acre most recently the 'market square' in Callendar Riggs, and of course the grand new Town Hall passed out of the hands of the Feuars who by then had effectively ceased to exist.

The new Court House, Burgh Buildings and Town Hall were all inspired by municipal authorities of one kind or another, but the independent commercial interests in the town were equally anxious to take a larger stake in an increasingly prosperous community. Nothing in Victorian Scotland demonstrated confidence and success more than fine, stone buildings in classical or baronial style and many were built in Falkirk. Thankfully, a goodly number have survived like the two built for the Royal Bank—David McGibbon's magnificent baronial building at the junction of Vicar Street and

Silver Row in the early years of the century not long before this particular section
nearest the High Street was demolished as unfit for human habitation.

Newmarket Street completed in 1863 and a similar design at west
end of the town by Peddie and Kinear in 1879. The former is now
an estate agent's and the latter the offices of the Northern Rock
Building Society. Elsewhere there was the Post Office building in
Vicar Street completed in 1893, the nearby red sandstone office of
the British Linen Bank from 1899, and the earliest of all the
Commercial Bank building on the High Street opposite the Cow
Wynd, opened in 1830. But as these monuments to prosperity
multiplied their magnificence must have been in stark contrast to
the prevailing squalor of the Back Row, the Howgate, Silver Row
and dozens of other dingy closes and courts. There, a rapidly
expanding population lived and worked at all manner of dirty and
dangerous occupations with little concern for health and public
safety and precious little sympathy or support from those who
prospered from their labours. The iron foundries which earned
fortunes for the masters offered unremitting, back-breaking labour
in the foulest of conditions and the coal mines and brick works
were just as bad. Only a genuine pride in the quality of the
workmanship compensated those thousands of men whose life
expectancy was cut short by their labours and that was far from
enough. The passing of the 1859 Improvement Act did strengthen

the hands of those who demanded change and a great deal was done in the decades which followed to tackle some of the most pressing problems, but another sixty years and a World War would pass before the worst of the housing slums were removed.

In the meantime the people had to survive as best they could and, sadly, many found relief from their labours at the bottom of a whisky glass in any one of dozens of Falkirk pubs which stood along the length of the High Street and from Newmarket Street to Bainsford Bridge. There was the Swan and the Cat, the Pie Office, the Red Lion and the Black Bull, the Kings Arms and the Crosskeys, whose most famous resident, the poet Robert Burns, visited the town in 1787. Many of these hosteries survived well into the modern era until the departure of the working population from the town centre to the outskirts brought about their gradual decline. At one time in the late 19th-century Falkirk was said to be second only to Airdrie as the most drunken town in Scotland and certainly the Sheriff Court reports in the Falkirk Herald testify to the truth of this particular claim to notoriety. But there were other entertainments! Sports of various kinds attracted a considerable following and if curling tended to be a major interest of the well-to-do then bowling had a more universal appeal and quoiting, pronounced 'kiting', absorbed whatever surplus energy the miners and moulders had left after their days graft. This was no namby-pamby pastime like the genteel game played on the deck of a luxury liner! The great cast-iron rings with built-in handles were hard enough to lift far less to throw, but throw them they did at iron pins set in clay beds on special 'kiting greens'. Miners from Plean tackled moulders from Carron in formal league matches before large crowds of spectators at the Boyd Street green, while lookouts watched for the 'Polis' lest the illegal side-bets were confiscated and the culprits marched off to the jail at the top of Hope Street. But in the end it was the football played at the other end of the street which won the hearts of most of the Falkirk faithful, though their East Stirlingshire rivals in Grahamston generated an amazing loyalty quite unrelated to their performances on the field. The 'Bairns' were established in 1876, the Shire five years later and while both began their existence in other parts of the town it is Brockville and Firs Park with which they will always be identified. These teams have specialised in breaking the hearts of their supporters for well over a century but like prodigal sons we forgive them again and again!

For those who disliked sporting activities 19th-century Falkirk offered the occasional dramatic presentation in places like the Assembly Rooms, Burns Court Hall or Wilson's Buildings. Often these took the form of colourful 'tableaux' saluting heroes like Nelson or General Gordon and glorifying the British Empire in words and song. As we have already seen the new Corn Exchange and Town Hall took over many of these activities from the mid-century on and great affairs like the annual Volunteer's Ball danced on 'a linen carpet' purchased from Wylie and Lockhead's in Glasgow, were the social highlights of the gentry's year.

The work of improving the town's environment continued to preoccupy the Town Council in the last quarter of the century. In the 1870s a new cemetery in Camelon more or less ended burials within the town and the opening of a new slaughter house in Kerse Lane in 1873 stopped the foul business of butchers killing animals in premises all over the burgh. But the provision of an adequate supply of fresh water was their single most important undertaking, though it was also the most costly and contentious.

Valiant attempts were made up to the early 1880s to extend and develop the supply of mine water from the traditional sources south of the town but with a much greater population now demanding up to ten gallons a day per head a new solution was required. Proposals were made and rejected, the ratepayers were consulted, the Provost and many councillors resigned, new proposals emerged and were rejected and old ones were unearthed, dusted down and offered once again! One account talks of a meeting held in the Town Hall to examine the proposals yet again in 1885 at which buckets of water from Summerford, Bells Meadow, Earls Burn and Faughlin were passed round and counsellors and ratepayers tasted the product for the sake of comparison. Later it was whispered that all had been filled in the horse trough outside the Hall but it mattered little. The decision—no decision!

The whole water saga was a classic example of the way in which local politicians went about their business during the period. Nothing was ever as simple as it looked and if it was it would not remain so for long! Eventually in 1888 the Falkirk and Larbert Water Trust emerged, charged with solving the problem and the same year settled on a small reservoir on the Faughlin burn near Carronside which would trap the water of the Denny Hills. From there the new supply would be piped via larger reservoirs and filter

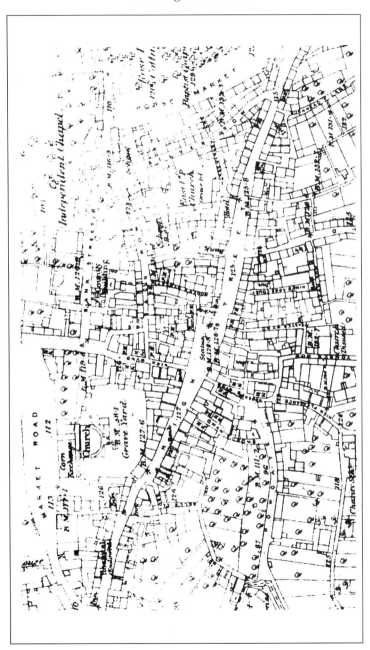

Falkirk in the 1860s from the first edition Ordnance Survey map

plants to the town. Agreement was reached and the work went ahead amid great enthusiasm. The scheme was officially opened in 1891 by the Duchess of Montrose and newspaper reports talk of great celebrations, triumphal arches and processions and small boys catching the water in their caps at the town wells and offering it to the adults in the vacinity. By the end of the century consumption had increased to over 40 gallons per head per day with many houses having their own piped supplies. But it would be well into the new century before the bulk of the population would be freed from dependance on town wells though at least now the quality and quantity matched the demand.

In 1870 the burgh was still marked out to east and west by open burns. The West Burn running from Gartcows to the foot of Cockburn Street, where it was known as Jenny Mair's, then east to Burnfoot Lane where it turned north to serve the tanneries in West Bridge Street or Tanner's Brae before continuing on towards the Carron. The East Burn arose to the south of the town in Callendar policies crossed to the main road at East Bridge Street, flowing north through the meadows to Lady's Mill where it had once powered one of the corn mills of the early barony. A third burn known as the Adam's Gote or Goat burn ran along past the Poorhouse, through Hodge Street to join the West Burn near the present Erskine Church. It was the discharge of sewage from the Poorhouse into the Goat which prompted a few gentlemen to gather subscriptions which eventually saw the West and Gote Burns piped underground in December 1870.

Another constant source of concern was the narrowness of most of the main streets of the burgh and from the mid 1850s through to the outbreak of the Great War in 1914 strenuous efforts were made by individuals as well as the authorities, to rectify the situation. The Cow Wynd was for centuries the principal road southwards from the town and successive generations condemned its inadequacy. At its junction with the High Street the Wynd was just 13 feet wide and one observer recalled that its surface was 'the dread of all who had to conduct vehicular traffic through it .... there is a tradition that more than once Carron coal carters threw down their whips declining to guide their horses through its miry way'. Little or nothing was done until the local newspapers turned their attention to the problem in the 1860s with the result that over a thousand tons of slag were rolled into the surface and covered by half as much again of whinstone. By then one of the dilapidated buildings at the High Street end had been removed and replaced by a new block, at the same time increasing the width to twenty feet.

Bad as the Cow Wynd had been it could not compare with the Back Row for human squalor and misery. At its junction with Kirk Wynd and for thirty yards eastwards it was only ten feet wide and was the first street to be tackled by the Town Council in its improvement campaign. Common lodging houses rickety old buildings, some dating from the 1600s, housed an assortment of immigrant labourers, street entertainers, second hand dealers, and public scavengers. The Town Council brought up properties on both sides of the street and after demolition a new building line was fixed. As the street slowly improved its ancient name was cast aside and Manor Street adopted in 1898. A rose by any other name indeed!

The first decade of the new century saw the same policy applied to the Kirk Wynd and Lint Riggs which was scarcely wide enough to allow a cart to pass through from the High Street to Newmarket Street. The Burgh Surveyor of the period David Ronald recalled his involvement in all these schemes in his memoirs. The state of some of the properties in the Lint Riggs made a particular impression on him.

> The rag store had an abundant colony of rats and on a wet day after a
> dry spell we used to look across from the Burgh Building to the store
> and count the number of rats drinking water in the rhone. Thirty was
> not an unusual number—we used to keep a record.

Again properties were bought, demolished and the street widened to its present condition, but it was becoming an expensive and time consuming activity with all manner of legal impediments to be overcome. A great deal remained to be done when war broke out in 1914 and plans were shelved for the time being.

The legacy of years of neglect which had inspired the proposers of the Act in 1859 had left Falkirk an easy prey to the ever present fevers which were the scourge of industrial Scotland in the last decades of the century. Infant mortality was high and life expectancy at birth low but improved water supplies and a start to slum clearance began to effect an improvement. But there were still

occasional threats from the deadly smallpox disease as the Falkirk
Mail of March 1888 testified:

> the public vaccinator Dr Peake will make a house to house visitation
> in the rural villages for the purpose of making enquiries as to parties
> requiring vaccination or re-vaccination and will perform such gratu-
> itously.

The same service was available in the town and the Sanitary Inspec-
tor set out to find those who failed to manage their 'piggaries,
dungsteads and privies' in a proper fashion. Despite these efforts
the dreaded disease appeared and the response was the building
of a hospital on the common land to the south of the town formerly
the property of the defunct Feuars. The small building put up in
less than a fortnight was the forerunner of the Fever Hospital, later
the Burgh or 'High' Hospital and now Lochgreen. The smallpox
patients were treated and within a few years the temporary structure had been replaced at a cost of over £9000 by the substantial
Fever Hospital treating typhoid, typhus and scarlet fevers as well as
diptheria until well into this century.

But sickness arising from non-infectious disease or as a result of
the frequent accidents in foundry and mine attracted no such
municipal action. For the victims there was little help available
beyond the support of a close community of fellow workers assisted
by the occasional generous doctor, prepared to offer free medicine
and treatment to the poorest and most defenceless. As the 18th
century wore on Victorian 'gentlemen and ladies' began to ac-
knowledge that their great wealth brought with it a duty to help
ameliorate the condition of the poorest in society, and by the 1880s
their efforts turned most often to the plight of the sick-poor.
Foremost among them was Mrs Harriet Gibson, wife of the owner
of Salton Ironworks, who was herself a regular visitor to the homes
of the sick in the town. In 1884 she appealed for help in the Falkirk
Herald:

> Let us hope that another year will not pass without our making an effort
> to have some place, though it were only one room with a few beds,
> where accidents could be attended to without causing the poor sufferer
> the added pain incurred by a journey from Edinburgh to Glasgow.

Although several years did pass before the proposal was taken up in earnest, she persisted and eventually won the support of many of her powerful and influential friends. An appeal was launched in October 1887 and soon over £1,300 had been collected or pledged. The following year the town's leading architect William Black was asked to design a new hospital with twelve beds around an existing cottage on a site in Thornhill Road. There was a furious response from local property owners who took the strongest possible exception to a hospital for the poor in their neighbourhood. A petition demanding a new site was circulated, and a vitriolic campaign supported by Mr Fred Johnston, proprietor and publisher of the Falkirk Herald got underway with an editorial blasting those 'secretive men' who, behind closed doors, had developed a scheme to site the hospital 'a respectable distance from Arnothill'

> The hospital has started very inauspiciously in having the opposition of the entire district in which it is to be placed and the adverse feeling of a large section of the general public who will be looked to for its future support.

But the project went ahead and by the summer the hospital was

The first Matron Miss Joss and her staff at the new Cottage Hospital in 1895.

ready. On Saturday 27th July 1889 before a 'large and brilliant gathering' watched by 'a curious crowd of spectators attracted by the long string of carriages', Mr Thomas Dawson Brodie declared the new Falkirk Cottage Hospital open. Much of the rancour which had accompanied the planning disappeared in the wave of enthusiasm with which the gentry of Falkirk greeted their new acquisition. Outside, as the last of the carriages departed, those less fortunate responded in like manner. 'In the evening', declared one observer, 'a very large number of the working classes inspected the building'. Twenty-four patients were treated in that first year and, as support from Doctors and the public increased, the numbers seeking admission multiplied so rapidly that within a few years an extension was required. In 1900 and again in 1906 successful appeals to the public allowed new buildings and more and more beds to be provided, so that almost 1000 'indoor and out-patients' were treated each year and over 600 operations performed in the splendid new operating room.

When Parochial Boards accepted responsibility in 1845 for the operation of a poor relief system the Falkirk Board calculated that it would need to raise £1400 each year to assist the poorest in the town. Four years later the figure was almost three times higher and in desperation the Board resolved to build a Poorhouse which

One of the first trams passing the Burgh buildings in 1906. The South African War Memorial is covered over prior to its unveiling by Lord Roberts in October of that year.

would reduce expensive outdoor relief as it was called, to manageable proportions. Land was obtained in Cow Wynd close to where Comely Park School now stands. The building was opened in January 1850 and soon after a section for 'lunatic paupers' was added. The Poorhouse served for over fifty years until the opening of a modern version, later Blinkbonny Home, in 1905 in the Gartcows area. Both buildings served the people of the town in various guises until their demolition—the Comely Park site became 'Woodside Home', a working men's hostel and eventually the County Trades School. It was removed in the 1980s. Blinkbonny was an old folks home between the wars and more recently Windsor Hospital. It was demolished in 1991.

Of course the ranks of the regular poor were quite often increased by the vagaries of trade or even the severity of the weather and in the dreadful winter of 1894 the country lay in the grip of freezing conditions for more than four months. In Falkirk the foundries were closed and the men laid off. Public works ground to a halt and the municipal authorities were forced to extreme measures to support the workers and their families. In December David Ronald, then working for the Burgh Engineer was ordered to establish a soup kitchen in the Burgh Stables across the road from the Poorhouse. Two large boilers formerly used for boiling food for the horses were employed and Ronald went out round the butchers and grocers of Falkirk collecting donations of meat, bones and cereals for the pot.

Tickets were issued by the Ministers of the town and two women were employed to make the soup. Soon over 100 people each day were queuing in High Station Road and as time passed it became more and more difficult to gather the necessary ingredients. David Ronald takes up the story.

> One day I was at the Slaughter house on some business and happened to mention my difficulty to the Superintendent. It was just a casual talk to start with, then he said 'Why should you not use the good part of the carcasses which have been condemned for tuberculosis?' The condemned carcasses at that time were buried behind the Slaughter House. I consulted the Medical Officer, Dr Griffiths, about the proposal, and he said that so long as the flesh was subjected to boiling-point temperature for about an hour, it would be all right, but that it would be better to say nothing about it, and so the meat problem was

solved. We still got a small quantity of meat from the butchers, but the
bulk of it came from the Slaughter House.

So popular was this concoction that the numbers doubled and at
the end of the day two old men came across with a pail and carried
the left over soup to the Poorhouse. No study has yet been done
on the incidence of tuberculosis in the years which followed but it
might make interesting reading!

No development symbolised the close of the old Victorian era
and the beginning of a bright, new age than the first electric power
generation in the town. In the 1890s several enterprising businessmen had installed electric generators to light their premises and
supply a few customers in and around the centre of the High Street.
At the great Free Church bazaar in 1896 in aid of funds for the
Newmarket Street church building, the Town Hall, Masonic Lodge
and the church were lit for three days by electricity as a novelty and
thousands of people came to see and wonder at the power of the
new age. In 1901 the Town Council decided that Falkirk should
have its own 'electric light' generating station and, despite the
contrary advice of the officials, opted for a building on land
adjacent to the Burgh Stables in High Station Road which they
owned already of course. The great coal fired boilers and the
generating dynamos were installed with a chimney over 120 feet
high dominating the south of the town. Many technical difficulties
had to be overcome and more than £25,000 was spent before the
first Falkirk electricity flowed to the shops, business premises and
occasional house in the town. Inevitably demand expanded rapidly
and the capacity of the plant was continually increased to provide
both light, heat and power throughout the burgh. But it was not
the Falkirk station which powered the town's most famous electricity user. When the electric trams first began their thirty year run
through the streets Bonnybridge Power Station, then owned by the
Tramway Company, was the monopoly supplier!

Before 1898 horsedrawn brakes and buses holding up to 36
passengers linked the town with the surrounding villages, but in
the spring of that year a local businessman formed the Falkirk and
District Motor Car Company Ltd with three eight seater Daimler
cars running from Falkirk to Stenhousemuir at half hourly intervals. In June 1898 they were following the familiar circular route
from Falkirk through Grahamston, Bainsford, Carron,

Stenhousemuir, Larbert and Camelon back to Falkirk. The Company was wound up two years later after a legal wrangle but by then proposals to cover the same route using electric trams were being prepared for Parliament's approval.

The major problem for the proposers was the need to replace the old wooden bascule bridges over the Forth and Clyde canal at Bainsford and Camelon and the stone bridge over the Carron close to the ironworks. Planning difficulties delayed the project and in 1904 the original proposers were replaced by a new company owned by Bruce Peebles, owners of the Scottish Central Electric Power Company which had been formed to provide power within the County of Stirling. They owned the new Bonnybridge station! Construction work began in January 1905 from Larbert Cross with rails laid to a unique 4 foot gauge with 21 double track loops to allow passing. The erection of the overhead power supply began in May the same year and progress was very rapid. The new Carron bridge cost nearly £4000 which the Town Council funded assisted by Carron and the Tramway Company; it was ready in September 1905. The Motherwell Bridge Company supplied the new turntable bridges for the canal crossings designed to open in under one minute to allow boats to pass through! Fifteen French built double-decker tramcars were in Falkirk by the autumn and on Sunday 21st October, members of the Town Council made the first circular journey through streets thronged by hundreds of enthusiastic Falkirk bairns. In 1909 the powers that be were once again celebrating—this time the departure of the first tram from Falkirk to Laurieston—a service which lasted until 1924. The major engineering work here had been the lowering of the road to allow the cars to pass beneath the Skew Bridge, though some widening in Falkirk High Street had also been necessary.

It was the beginning of a love affair for Falkirk people for seldom has an institution provoked such retrospective affection and sincere regret at its untimely demise in 1936. But that was a long time in the future. In the first year of operation over 3½ million passengers were carried and though the figure did reduce from this very high figure the trams were firmly established as the major mode of transport within the Falkirk area. The cheap and swift service now available to the people in the villages brought them in droves to the shopping centre of Falkirk which rapidly resumed its traditional role as the market centre of east Stirlingshire. A glance

Newmarket Street around 1900 looking east showing the Town Hall and Free
Church on the right hand side.

through the trade directories for the period reveals the wealth of
choice awaiting the visitors; lovers of 'my Lady Nicotine'were invited to visit the High Street premises of James Clarkson, while the
musicians could find 'everything from a pipe organ to a penny
whistle' at Sowdan and Forgan's shop in Vicar Street. Health
enthusiasts might try Thomas Lyon's 'crebanus borax and eucalyp-
tus soap', visit Alexander McDonald the 'tonsorial artist' where the
'hair brushing is done by machinery' or even pass an hour or two
at the new Waverley Public Wash-house and Baths in the Howgate
described as 'a much desiderated convenience, and a marvel of
moderation in respect of tariff'. But when it came to serving the
inner man Falkirk really came into its own. There was Mrs Tod's
shop in the High Street where the 'smoked hams have a reputation
all of their own and are sliced for the purchaser with a skill that
provokes admiration' and not far away 'the denizens of the deep'
were laid out for inspection on the spacious slabs of Sutherland's
fishmongers shop. Under the Steeple stood Brodie's popular
butchers shop and patrons were reminded that it was Mr Brodie
himself who had helped introduce a painless cattle killer to the
Falkirk slaughter-house 'a fact which speaks volumes for his hu-
mane disposition'! Those with a few pounds to spend and an eye
for high technology might purchase a bicycle called the 'Brockville'

Brodie's butcher shop at the bottom of the steeple just before the First World War.

manufactured by Malley's or even a collapsible one man turkish bath from Millers of Vicar Street.

Most of the shops have long since ceased to trade in the town but there were some like Zuill and Stewart, Dillon's, Anderson's and Alexander's Stores which were operating until comparatively recently and one or two still serve the people of the town nearly a century later. Inglis' printers, and Malley's are still going strong along with Mr R Mathieson's bakery and tearooms which around 1900 were 'the happy hunting ground of weary commercials and hungry farmers, and, in the summer months of whildom batchelor or grass widower, when sea-side attractions take mothers and wives away' But all too soon it was not the wives and mothers, but the sons, fathers and brothers who were away, this time far from the sands of Ayr or Portobello, but among the mud and rain of Flanders fields. The optimism with which Falkirk had entered the new century perished along with much else there, and those fortunate enough to return safely found a different town and a much changed world waiting for them.

CHAPTER 10

Falkirk in the 20th Century

The outbreak of war with Germany in August 1914 brought the fever of public works in the burgh to an abrupt halt. In common with villages and towns throughout the land, Falkirk people devoted themselves to the business of supporting the war effort by whatever means was most appropriate to their particular talents and situation. The rush to the colours among young men was as marked in the district as anywhere else and the Falkirk Herald reported amazing scenes just days after war was declared:

> The Patriotic Spirit has spread like wildfire and the rush of intending recruits has been so great that at times it has been impossible to cope fully with it. To facilitate the work an office has been procured in West Bridge Street where the men desirous of serving King and Country may have themselves enrolled as defenders of the Empire. The scenes witnessed at the West Bridge Street Office have been nothing short of remarkable; for hours at a stretch the eager volunteers for service forming lengthy queues in front of the premises

Hundreds of territorials were called up and trains from Grahamston Station carried them off to an uncertain future though the popular slogan 'home for Christmas' deceived few who understood the nature of modern warfare. War office orders for shells and other munitions poured into the Falkirk foundries and business boomed as it had in the Napoleonic and Crimean Wars of earlier centuries. Church groups threw themselves into a frenzy of fund raising, gathering parcels full of comforts for the troops and knitting socks and scarves galore for the men at the front. The nurses and doctors in Falkirk's new Infirmary prepared to treat the war wounded but found the bulk of their time given to the needs of territorial men recruited in the district who were not immediately fit for active service. In the first six months for example, nearly 200 men were in-patients suffering from anaemia, sciatica,

Women at work making munitions for Falkirk Iron Company.
Courtesy John Walker.

rheumatism, haemorrhoids, varicose veins, flat feet, hammer toes, scabies and eczema and the surgeon conducted '62 operations on soldiers to fit them for active service and 50 to enable men to enlist'. But soon the overseas men with gunshot and shrapnel wounds began to arrive and the impact of the real war began to sink in. Over 1100 men from Falkirk burgh were lost as the mindless carnage on the western front dragged on and on. And who knows how many thousands more fell beneath the iron rain of shells made by the decent, honest men and women of Falkirk? It was the nature of the age and those who worked over here and fought over there believed in what they did with little reservation. When it was all over they mourned their losses, honoured the survivors and celebrated their contribution to the victory. But by then many of them understood.

In 1919 the Falkirk Iron Company published a remarkable series of photographs showing young women working in Castle Laurie Foundry making all kinds of bombs and shells, and they remain as a chilling reminder of the foundation of much of Falkirk's prosperity. In the same year returning soldiers were honoured by the Town Council for their service while congregations and town officials laid plans for permanent memorials to the fallen. Several

The World War 1 Certificate of Honour Awarded to Private James Morton by the Burgh of Falkirk in 1919. *Courtesy* Robert McLaughlin.

years were to pass before these were ready—in April 1923, for example, a packed congregation in the Parish Church witnessed the dedication of a memorial stone canopy with the names of 97 members of the congregation who perished. Each name was solemnly read aloud by the Minister—the husbands, sons and fathers of the congregation. Even after sixty odd years the description of that service never fails to move and chill in equal measure. And it was a scene repeated in every church in the town as the people came to terms with their loss. The Town Council chose a cenotaph situated on the Camelon Road in Dollar Park designed by local architect Leonard Blakey and unveiled in 13th June 1926 by the Duke of Montrose. Every year since that day the men of Falkirk have been remembered—'Over 1100 Falkirk bairns died for their King and country and in the cause of Freedom'. Elsewhere in the district 18 memorials were raised—crosses, obelisks and plain blocks of stone each one a reminder to a village of its sacrifice.

With the ending of munitions contracts the foundries struggled to restore their order books and short time working and layoffs were the inevitable result. The women who had turned their hands to moulding in the emergency found themselves back in the ill-paid drudgery of pre-war years and shortages of basic foodstuffs made life extremely difficult. But things slowly improved and by the 1920s industry was once again strong and prospects brighter. In 1925 one trade union official claimed that the light castings industry was in a most prosperous condition better than for 25 years. There was not an unemployed iron worker in the district or so he said. This was due in no small measure to Government action on housing in 1919 following a Royal Commission report on the state of housing in Scotland, reinforced by the Housing Act of 1925. which funded municipal authorities to clear slums and build new houses. Over 500 new houses were built in the Burgh up to 1927 and since over three quarters of the output of the Falkirk foundries went into producing ranges, baths, water pipes and grates, the housing boom meant security for Falkirk's workforce as well as substantial new houses for themselves and their families. Even the General Strike of 1926 when the local coal mines were closed for many months, did not seriously disrupt the output. Although 8,000 people gathered in Victoria Park to hear the famous miner's leader A J Cook speak on the strike, the Falkirk moulders remained at work. New gas fired plant and imported coal sustained the foundries and the

The moulding shop in Carron Works in the early years of the century.

crisis passed. But within a few years with a new Conservative Government reducing the housing subsidies demand again began to fall and 1928 and 1929 saw short time working, wage reductions and a strike involving 2,000 men. Business men in the area were alarmed and together launched the Falkirk, Grangemouth and East Stirlingshire Development Association with the express aim of attracting new industry to the area by stressing the availability of land, skilled labour and good communications. Seventy years on and the message is the same!

In 1922 Cockburn's Gowanbank Foundry had formed a grouping with several English iron works and now with the industry under pressure, the group expanded to twenty-three and became Allied Ironfounders. Seven of the firms were in the Falkirk area including the giant Falkirk Iron Company with over 1,000 workers, Cockburn's, Callendar Abbots, Forth and Clyde, Sunnyside and Dobbie Forbes. The object of the merger was to allow specialisms to develop and reduce wasteful competition and in this it was successful for most of the Falkirk components survived and prospered until the middle of this century. The second Labour Government of 1929 produced yet another Housing Act and once again the Falkirk Council pressed on with slum clearance, new building and once more the foundries were the beneficiaries.

A new town began to take shape as the worst of the town centre

Three of the 1930s buildings from the town centre - the shops and apartments in Cockburn Street, the former Co-operative Store in Kirk Wynd and the Cannon Cinema in Princes Street. *Photographs* Michael Middleton.

slums were emptied and pulled down and new housing schemes rose up on the fringes of the old burgh boundaries. Merchiston Avenue, the Millflats and Thornhill areas and Carmuirs in Camelon were gradually covered by new buildings and by the mid 1930s a plan for a further 800 houses was approved. The Bog Road scheme was the last to start before war once again slowed down material supplies and reduced the progress to a snail's pace. By then the High Street had been widened by the demolition of the east end including a substantial part of the dreadful Silver Row. The Callendar Riggs had been totally transformed and a new street bearing the name was cut through the hill. Millions of tons of sand and earth were removed in the process and modern shops were erected along its length with a bus depot owned by the rapidly expanding Walter Alexander Company established behind them. Next to this, according to one observer 'is in course of erection a palatial terpsichorean hall by Mr John Doak, the well known Falkirk dancing expert'- in terms of significance for the future well being of the town and its people, this new arrival was surely as important as any new steeple, bank or store!

Elsewhere two new streets were formed. In 1933 Newmarket Street was joined to Park Street and the east of the town by Prince's Street opened by the Prince of Wales, the future King Edward VIII. The previous year the High Street at the west end had been opened up to allow a new road to the south to be created which joined Cockburn Street near the bottom of the Howgate. New streets meant new buildings in the style of the period and Falkirk has several fine examples of art deco from the 1930s—the great ocean-liner shape of the Grand Theatre in Prince's Street later the Regal Cinema and now the Cannon; the bow-ended shops and flats in Cockburn Street and the restored Co-operative Super Store in Kirk Wynd, now the Clydesdale Bank. Then there is the bus station itself and Doak's building as well as Young's Stores in Princes Street, now Rosie O'Grady's and the office of the Allied Iron Founders in Graham's Road—a rich harvest indeed from that last great period of design before the wheels came off in the fifties and sixties. There was a new school too, the 'educational palace' of the Technical School, now Graeme High opened in 1932 and at long, long last, a public baths replacing that good and faithful servant, the Assembly Rooms in the Pleasance. These new baths were themselves demolished in 1989.

The building with the least pretension to architectural merit was the new Infirmary opened by Prince George in January 1932 in front of thousands of celebrating bairns. Behind its plain and practical facade lay one of the most remarkable stories in the whole history of the Falkirk district. The old Thornhill Infirmary had been extended several times and still could not cope with the demands for its services. By 1922 nearly 1000 patients had been treated with twice as many outpatients and 900 operations. The experts advised a new hospital in a new site and so began an incredible decade of fundraising involving people of every rank in the community. The present site at Gartcows was purchased for around £6,000 and on 27th April 1925 over a thousand people crammed the Town Hall for the official launch of the Great Appeal.

It was the prelude to an astonishing five year spell in which every conceivable method of fund-raising was employed, and hardly an organisation or individual failed to participate whether wittingly or not. If they attended a play or pantomime, part of the receipts went to the fund. The same applied to football matches and dances, school concerts and bus trips, picnics and whist drives. There were collecting boxes everywhere—outside hospital wards, in public buildings, in private houses, in shops and business premises. The overwhelming impression which comes through from newspaper articles and official reports, concert programmes and souvenirs is of a great and happy collaboration of all the people of the district in securing 'their' Infirmary. Every square yard of the site, every brick of the buildings, every stick of furniture and equipment and every penny of wages and salaries would be provided by the people. 'Touch ane, Touch a' proclaimed the Infirmary motto, and the response was the most eloquent proof of the truth of its message.

A glance through the local newspaper for 1926 and '27 reveals a frenzy of fund-raising activity. One might for example, enjoy 'The Merchant of Venice' at the Dobbie Hall, ' Floradora' in the Grand Theatre, or 'She Stoops to Conquer' in the Town Hall. There was a 'Fancy Fair' and '6d. bazaar' in the YMCA hut, 'Mr Martin's Orchestra Dance' in the Gymnasium, Camelon, 'Music in the Garden' at Arnothill, a 'Vocal Recital' in the Masonic Temple and a 'Palais de Danse' in the Temperance Cafe. For sporting types there were football, cricket and tennis competitions as well as the chance to see a 'Great Boxing Gala in Jim Paterson's new and commodious Pavilion' to see 'a four round contest between

Spowart's midgets' along with Falkirk's own 'Fatty Wells, Young Connell and Butcher Anderson'. There were road races, grand penny trails, watch-winding competitions, highland gatherings, popular lectures, community singing, open days at mansion houses, jumble sales and silver paper collections. There were official 'Infirmary Weeks' with great carnivals of students in fancy dress and decorated floats parading through the streets of the town. The list was endless. A small book was produced entitled 'Seventy Three Ways in Which You Can Help Your Infirmary' and it included as number 32:

> Strap onto your dog a collecting box and teach him to make collections—but not in public thoroughfares without a special permit

The collecting boxes themselves were novel—one shaped like a brick exhorted 'Be a Brick—fill a Brick', while the other showed a patient in bed with a message 'Never Pass Me By'. Sufficient bricks were filled and the boxes seldom passed by. By the time the Duchess of Montrose cut the first sod of Gartcows in November 1926 the fund had reached nearly £90,000, well within sight of the target. In the Autumn of 1928 the new Infirmary appeal was brought to an end by a 'Grand Bazaar' which would, it was hoped raise the final £5,000 required. For four days great crowds flocked to the Drill Hall where stall holders from all over the district sold their wares. When the last penny was counted the astonishing total raised was £9,600, the largest sum ever achieved by bazaar in a Scottish provincial town. Today's equivalent figure would be close to £200,000! By the end of 1930 the new building was ready for inspection and in two weeks in December nearly 8,000 visitors did just that.

The patients moved to the new Infirmary at the beginning of 1931 and a year later Prince George officially declared the building open in front of 20,000 people. It had cost in total £120,000—nearly £3 million by today's standards—and was opened free of debt. There were 85 beds, served by 45 nursing staff—five years later it was 200 beds and 75 nursing staff. And the astonishing growth went on and on.

The list of activities which helped to provide funds for the Infirmary gives something of the flavour of entertainment in the town in the first half of the 20th-century. A fine tradition in amateur drama developed and remains strong today, and high quality operatic and choral societies provided an outlet for the abundant talents of the local community. The pubs which had such a hold on Victorian 'bairns' were still there in abundance of course but now there were picture houses all over the town and surrounding district. Like all of Scotland Falkirk went movie-mad!. The Grand Theatre became Falkirk's 'super cinema', later the Regal, now the Cannon. Then there was the Pavilion, later called the Gaumont, opposite the brewery in Newmarket Street. At the other end was the Salon and round the corner in Melville Street, the Cinema. Finally the Picture House in Bank Street which, as we have seen, began life as a church and now hosts the bingo! Outside the town Camelon had the Ritz, there was the La Scala in Grangemouth, the Picture Palace in Stenhousemuir and the Picture House in Brightons among others. The Roxy Theatre in Silver Row which had for a time operated under the name the Electric Theatre, continued to bring the cream of Scottish variety to the town until television killed off that particular art form in the 1950s.

Dancing was tremendously popular with Doak's Dancing Academy (Ladies one shilling, Gentlemen one-and-six), the Burlington in Cow Wynd, and Mathieson's New Ballroom in the High Street where Saturday night patrons danced to the Manhattan Band. Boxing matches filled the Town Hall and the Ice-Rink offered skating and Ice Hockey to large and enthusiastic crowds. Football continued to be the most popular spectator sport with twenty-thousand not an unusual Saturday gate at Brockville. The Falkirk Bairns brought home the Scottish Cup twice, in 1912 and in 1957 to the univeral delight of the towns-people, football fans or not. The Shire's main claim to national fame was a brief move away from Falkirk to Clydebank of all places in the 1960s and a subsequent bitter and successful battle led inevitably by James Middlemass to bring the team back to the town.

The decades after the first war brought mixed fortunes to the burgh's tramway system. Regular motorbus services challenged the monopoly and the Tramway Company responded by acquiring buses of its own to cover routes away from its established lines. A programme of track reconstruction with all the dislocation and expense involved began in 1921 and the circular route was not completed for eight years. Soon after ten new single decker trams were introduced and much of the business lost during the reconstruction phase was regained. Despite that the death knell was already sounding. Cut throat competition from bus companies and takeovers and mergers were the order of the day and in 1935 the shareholders were bought out by the Scottish Motor Traction Company. By the summer of the following year the brand new trams were sold, the track lifted and the whole system consigned to a premature place in the history books. On 21st July 1936 the last of the trams carried a floral wreath. Many mourned their passing and still do—over fifty years later. At the time of writing the city fathers in Glasgow have announced their intention of restoring the trams—maybe the lesson will not be lost on those who shape the destiny of this part of the world!

The outbreak of war in 1939 for the second time in a generation provoked none of the wild enthusiasm of the first great conflict. Grim determination was the message emerging from the pages of the Falkirk Herald as people throughout the district prepared for what all expected—swift bombing raids on all centres of population. A year before the war the situation had provoked the authorities to issue gas masks and now they were to be carried everywhere. Blackouts were introduced immediately and street lamps extinguished. At Brockville Park the players were advised to find jobs— no play, no pay was the motto—and children from, Glasgow began to arrive in numbers at Grahamston Station on their way to Muiravonside, Polmont and other villages. People began to construct their own shelters and the Town Council stung by repeated criticism of their tardiness laid plans for public shelters including one in New Market Street gardens. Volunteers dug up tons of sand in Bell's Meadow which went to fill the bags now stacked round key buildings. But the bombers stayed away and the slow realisation that they would not be coming in the immediate future began to change the approach. Football was back on again within a few weeks and the population settled back into a home front routine reminiscent of 1914-18. This time men were conscripted into the fighting services and women were involved for the first time. Large numbers of Falkirk men and women received their papers and left for training centres throughout the land. Church halls and some school premises were taken over by the military and at the Royal Infirmary twelve huts were erected as special wards for the expected rush of civilian and military casualties. Those who stayed did what was asked of them—men who were in protected

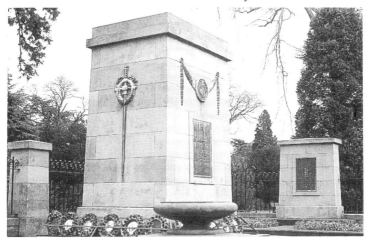

The Dollar Park War Memorial first dedicated in 1926.
Photograph Geoff Bailey.

occupations in munitions or mining or essential services , or who were too old to serve, joined the Home Guard, or ARP, or special Fire Services. And once again the church groups began the fund raising, sewing bees, jumble sales and basket teas which produced thousands of parcels for Falkirk men in the services.

As the War progressed and the immediate fear of bombing receded, the new nightmare was that the Germans would invade and occupy the country. In Falkirk the local press warned 'Herr Hitler' that his stormtroopers could expect a pretty tough reception if they made the mistake of marching in the Callendar Road. The people of the town were urged to put their savings in Defence and War Bonds and support War Weapons Weeks like that which took place in February 1941 when military units, ARP, Home Guard, and youth organisations paraded through the town to the Burgh Buildings where Lord Rosebery took the salute. Even after the success of the Battle of Britain the belief persisted that the enemy were biding their time and that a great blitz followed by an invasion was on the cards. As part of the defence Falkirk people were urged to contribute to a fund to purchase a Spitfire to be known as the 'Falkirk Bairn'. Eventually over £10,000 was subscribed and the plane was presented to the Royal Air Force in 1941.

The war ground on, years of digging for victory, of dried eggs and powdered milk, blackouts, air raid shelters and gas masks, ration books and clothing coupons and mince made from oatmeal. It was a world which for all its hardship had a profound influence on the lives of the people of Falkirk who lived through it. When it was over they celebrated in great style and the troops were welcomed home with special events throughout the district. Once again the burgh's loss was mourned at the cenotaph—'On the sea, in earth's distant places and in the air nearly 220 men and women of Falkirk died for their country in the cause of righteousness'.

The fifty years since the end of the war rival the equivalent period of the last century for the intensity of the clearing and rebuilding which so much changed the look of the town. Unfortunately for many, the architects and the materials they chose to employ, combined to produce a new townscape of unrelieved dullness which is only now giving way to design and planning in keeping with the feel of the old burgh. Once the inevitable material shortages of the post war period were overcome the Council turned its attention once more to the housing situation. By 1947 the population of the burgh was given as 32,000 and there were around 10,000 houses with a third of them described as overcrowded and nearly 2,000 unfit for human habitation. Worse still, 3,431 people were on the waiting list for a council house, and plans were approved which would provide 2,000 new houses of three apartments or bigger. Soon land at Cobblebrae in Carron, East Carmuirs in Camelon and Windsor Road was acquired and construction work started. In addition the pre-war Bog Road scheme continued.

But this time the housing boom was no lifeline for the foundries—technology and taste had changed and new materials filled the kitchens and bathrooms of the huge housing schemes—and the slow decline began to accelerate. Camelon and Callendar Abbots were the first to go in the 1950s, followed by Etna, Carmuirs, Forth and Clyde, R and A Main and Grange in the 60s, Cockburns in the 70s, and finally the two giants Carron and Falkirk Iron Company in the early 80s. The last one in the town, Grahamston, closed in 1994 and of the dozens of foundries in east Stirlingshire in 1940 only a handful were still operating fifty years later. With them went highly successful firms like Towers who manufactured refractory bricks, and a host of smaller companies in engineering whose living depended on the success of the iron moulders.

The effects of this decline on jobs were offset to some extent by the arrival of new industry. In 1944 the Government Ministry responsible for producing aircraft, erected an aluminium rolling mill on a site north of the Forth and Clyde canal in Bainsford. Two years later with the peace assured, the plant was taken over by the British Aluminium Company and in the years that followed production of plate, sheet and strip increased dramatically in response to the demand for the 'new' material from architects, engineers and interior designers. Massive investment in new manufacturing equipment made the plant one of the most important in the kingdom and by the mid sixties over 2,500 men and women were employed on the sixty acre site. Former ironworkers and their families found new security in the modern surroundings of the plant and on the land of Langlees to the north, a huge new housing estate developed.

The phenomenal growth of the petro-chemical complex at Grangemouth will be described in the next chapter and this, along with British Aluminium, the expansion of Alexander's coach building works in Camelon and the development of a host of other enterprises including printing and bookbinding, saved the town from potential disaster. Many suffered in the process of change but Falkirk as a community survived the trauma which the collapse of the staple industry had threatened. Two long established businesses on the town centre were on the move in the period. James Aitken's Brewery eventually fell foul of the takeovers and mergers of the 1960s and after a short period as part of Caledonian United, later Tennent Caledonian, Breweries, production was run down and brewing ceased in 1966. Four years later the famous chimney came down and the huge site was developed as the present supermarket and a carpark.

On the other side of the west-end junction at Burnfoot, Scotland's other national drink, Barrs Irn Bru, was proving so popular that no further expansion was possible. In May 1971 the old site was abandoned and a large modern factory costing half a million pounds was opened at Hopedale in Camelon near Lock 16, where it continues to prosper today. The old place at Burnfoot is now a roundabout.

Carparks and roundabouts—it was indicative of the new age of the car which came to dominate the planners' thinking in the decades since the war. When the last of Falkirk's old and outmoded houses were pulled down in the 60s and 70s—in the Garrison, Glasgow buildings and the Howgate—car parks appeared in their place. When new buildings were erected they were mainly commercial ones like the new Callendar Centre at the east end of the High Street which was hailed as a modern marvel but which most people disliked from day one. Many of the old stores on the south west of the High Street were replaced by modern facades so utterly bereft of style that one wondered what fate the planners had in mind for the old town. Large department stores with long frontages spelled the end for many familiar closes and wynds—Burns Court and Swords Wynd vanished forever and Falkirk, smarter no doubt, was the poorer for their disappearance.

The new Town Hall and Municipal Buildings at the bottom of Tanner's Brae, though ultra modern in design and further evidence of the 'tyranny of the right angle', had the virtue of standing well away from the old town centre in a setting which helped to ease the pain! And there is no doubt that the steady growth in municipal power this century meant that such new facilities were essential. The same applied to the Post Office which was, by the 1970s, too small; a new building across the road next to Grahamston Station replaced the familiar Victorian building in Vicar Street, which has mercifully survived the bulldozers. But there were some fine examples of modern planning and development to set alongside the disasters. When Callendar House and grounds

The new Technical College opened in 1961. It is now Falkirk College of Technology, the fifth largest of its kind in Scotland.

were acquired by the Town Council from the Forbes family in the early 60s the area was developed as a public park, with a number of high rise buildings set along the line of the Callendar Road. There can be few developments of type in Central Scotland in such a beautiful setting and they remain a model for all the others. The jewel of Callendar House itself was left to rot by a generation more concerned with solving immediate problems than protecting their inheritance. It was understandable—unforgivable, but understandable.

New school buildings were provided throughout the town, offering up to date facilities in keeping with developments in education—Bantaskine, Easter Carmuirs, St Francis, St Andrews and Langlees Primaries and St Mungo's Secondary, later High School, in Bainsford were opened from the 1950s on and in, 1961, Falkirk High School moved from Rennie Street after 63 years to new buildings in Bantaskine.

But it was the education of those beyond school age which attracted the biggest investments in the period. Falkirk had campaigned for a new University in East Stirlingshire in the early 60s but lost out to Stirling. In September 1964 came the compensation—a new college in Callendar estate as part of a nationwide expansion of teacher training. At one stage it had many hundreds of students but regrettably it did not survive the cutbacks of the 1980s and closed its doors after less than twenty years. The site was cleared and no trace of the building now remains. A much more permanent development was the million pound Falkirk Technical College on the Grangemouth Road, officially opened in 1962. Four centres in the Falkirk area had trained apprentices for the engineering, foundry, mining and building trades since the war and in the 1950s the Education Authority decided on the bold plan of building an integrated Further Education centre on one site. By the end of the decade it had nearly 5,000 students and 140 staff.

When local government was reorganised in 1975 Falkirk and Grangemouth Town Councils were absorbed into a new Falkirk District Council within Central Region. It was the end of more than a century of expansion and decline, hardship and prosperity and never ending change.

CHAPTER 11

The Villages

All over east Stirlingshire small settlements have grown up over the centuries into substantial villages or prosperous towns and their history is every bit as fascinating as that of Falkirk itself. Here we can only sketch the outline of these stories and must inevitably concentrate on those places lying nearest to the town. Thus the old and historic port of Airth, the iron and paper town of Denny and its neighbour across the Carron at Dunipace, Bonnybridge astride the canal, Slamannan and the rest of the villages to the south are not included. On the other hand Camelon, Larbert and Stenhousemuir, Grangemouth and Polmont are here because their development is very closely linked to that of Falkirk's own and their direct influence on the history of the whole area has been of very great significance.

Camelon

Of these villages, Camelon has most exercised the imaginative power of antiquaries and local historians over the years. A mighty Roman harbour, a great Pictish city with twelve brass gates, battles galore involving Pict and Scot, Angle and Briton and, of course, the Camelot and round table of King Arthur himself—all have had their champions and such theories continue to appear regularly even in this more sceptical age. Alas for romance, the evidence for such past glory is scant or non-existent and this is not the place to reinforce such fancy. The truth is interesting enough by any standard.

We have already encountered the great fort built by the Romans during their brief but eventful occupation in the second century. The military road which crossed the Antonine Wall at Watling Lodge passed the fort before crossing the Carron at Larbert—it is certainly possible that the river was navigable as far as Camelon

during the Roman period and may well have been used as the point
of entry and departure for men and materials during the years of
occupation and campaigning. But whether there was a harbour or
not the north road was important enough to demand a heavily
garrisoned fort in its defence and if Roman positions were indeed
attacked by tribal enemies then Camelon would have been an
obvious target.

After the Romans withdrew from the area for the last time the
place we now know as Camelon disappeared from the record for
close on fifteen hundred years. Only with the coming of the new
age of iron and the cutting of the Great Canal in the 18th Century
does the village emerge from the darkness and have an existence
which we can identify and describe with any certainty. The stretch
of the canal from Bainsford through the farmland of Camelon was
completed in the early 1770s and soon attracted manufacturers and
traders who recognised the benefits of a swift and dependable
transport system. The Lock 16 area, and the junction point where
the road from Falkirk dipped under the canal, quickly became
growth points and there were no doubt storehouses, loading basins
and stables serving the growing canal traffic from quite an early
stage. By the beginning of the 19th century the village population
was reported to be close to 600 and growing with a considerable
number engaged in the manufacture of nails.

It is William Cadell, son of Carron's founder and himself the
first manager of the works, who is credited with the establishment
of the earliest nailmaking concern in Camelon. In 1790, more than
twenty years after he gave up a direct interest in the works at
Carron, Cadell brought a group of skilled nailmakers from England to begin manufacturing in the village. The Cadells had bought
out Carron's interest in this particular activity in the 1770s and had
already established workshops in Bannockburn and Laurieston as
well as places much further afield. In Camelon the trade expanded
steadily and young men were drawn to the area and apprenticed
to masters who taught them the secrets of a hard, heavy and ill
rewarded trade. Houses, workshops, tools and nailrods were supplied by Cadell to the men and to the boys, often no more than
nine or ten years old, who slaved for twelve or more hours each
day to turn out the thousands of nails that were required to earn
a living wage:

George Square in Camelon, centre of one of the earliest nail making
establishments.

round the central fire hammered away four nailers. ..... no rest, no
breathing space for them. From hour to hour the bent back and steady
quick stroke, for the nailer must strike when the iron was hot and he
had to pay for heating the iron. In the morning they hied to the
warehouse for their bundles of rods which were converted into nails
ranging in length from ½ inch to 12 inches.

Four nailer's rows or squares appeared in Camelon—the Wee
Square at the west end, Fairbairn's Square, owned by George
Fairbairn, a leading nailmaster of the early 19th century, George
Square close to Lock 16 on the canal and Gunn's Square in the
same vacinity. Living conditions were extremely poor and the
nailers and their families developed a reputation for hard living
and hard drinking, which survived until mechanical nailmaking
robbed them of a living from the middle of the century on. One
observer in 1840 thought things were improving:

> The morals of the nailmakers have been improved within the last few
> years. In particular drunkenness and habits of improvidence are greatly
> on the decrease.

By then a visit of the dreaded cholera in 1833 had brought many
deaths to the nailer's rows with Mr Harrison paying £40 to assist

with the burial costs 'which has been repaid from the earnings of survivors'. After this, a penny-a-week death fund was established to offer the vulnerable nailers some protection.

The completion of the Union Canal in 1822 confirmed Camelon's status as the fulcrum of the new communication system and soon new inns, workshops, storage facilities and houses appeared along the banks and basins of Port Downie. By 1831 the population was over 800 rising within a decade to 1,340. Sometime around 1840 two brothers from Airth, James and Andrew Ross began building boats in a yard near Lock 16; after only five years Andrew was dead and young James who had discovered the value of pitch as a commodity in the boatyard moved into chemical manufacture at Limewharf just a few hundred yards west of Port Downie. Crude tar from various gas works was shipped to Camelon where it was converted into naphtha, pitch and refined tar. Business boomed and James Ross directed the expanding company for thirty years until 1878 when Robert Sutherland and Robert Orr assumed control. New products multiplied—sulphate of ammonia, benzine, creosote, and toluene, a key ingredient in the manufacture of TNT explosives—and prosperity followed. The firm did well during the years of war but in 1929, the same year as the sore pressed iron foundries were forming the Allied, the Lime Wharf Chemical Works became part of Scottish Tar Distillers. It survived until a disastrous fire in 1973 destroyed the works and soon afterwards all production on the site came to an end.

By the end of the Victorian era a number of chemical companies had followed James Ross into business in Camelon and were employing hundreds of men in the manufacture of sulphuric acid, iodine, and dozens of other compounds by then in high demand in the rapidly expanding Scottish economy. The Hurlet Works (1851), Camelon Chemical Works (1878) and Crosses (1900) flourished briefly but never attained the prosperity of Lime Wharf though they did help bring the infant chemical industry to the Falkirk district where it would reach its full flowering in the Grangemouth developments of the present century.

From the start the people of Camelon village looked for the services which confirmed their status as a new community. As part of Falkirk Parish they depended on the Minister there for their spiritual needs and on the heritors for the provision of education. In 1786 a rented house paid for by subscription among the

The two canals were linked by a series of locks and pools which provided the
children of Camelon with outdoor swimming facilities! The Kings Bridge carried
the railway over the Union Canal but the locks, pools and bridge have long since
disappeared.

villagers, was converted to a schoolroom and five years later a
'thatched but and ben' was built on land feued from Forbes of
Callendar. Thus in 1797 the Minister of Falkirk could report that
'in the village of Camelon there is a dwelling house and schoolroom for the encouragement of a schoolmaster, but no salary'. The
establishment of the 'School and Well Committee' in 1799 to
maintain what were seen as the community's principal or only
assets, was another example of the villagers' willingness to band
together to fight for the common good of all, a tendancy which
has marked the people of Camelon in all the years since then. The
Committee appointed seven 'stint-masters' from their number and
while they found it as difficult as their opposite numbers in Falkirk,
to raise the sums due, the school did continue to grow and the
teacher's salary was usually paid. Sometimes though, their poverty
was to his disadvantage as in 1847 when the Committee resolved
that 'all the panes of glass awanting in the school to be replaced
by the teacher', later clarified as 'such glass as is broken in school
hours'. A new school building was provided in 1874 but it proved
to be too small and a much larger building, the present Carmuirs
primary was opened by the Parochial Board in 1901.

 The explosion of iron founding in the district in the second half

of the 19th century had a major impact on Camelon and again the
Forth and Clyde canal had a great deal to do with the choice of
site. The first was established in 1845 near Lock 16 and was known
variously as Port Downie or Camelon Iron Works. It survived until
the 1950s. It was followed by the Union (1854-1879), the Forth and
Clyde (1870-1963), R and A Main's Gothic Works (1899-1964),
Grange (1900-1960s), Carmuirs (1899-1968) and Dorrator founded
in 1898 which survived until very recent times—it finally closed in
the late summer of 1994. At their height in the years before the
first war the Camelon foundries employed over 1,300 men manufacturing the familiar range of domestic and industrial ironware
including grates, stoves, pipes, cookers, gates, fences and
mantlepieces.

The rapid growth in the population increased demands for a
church in Camelon and, with the support of the Minister of Falkirk
William Begg and William Forbes of Callendar who provided a site
free of charge, a new building was erected at the west end of the
village to the design of Edinburgh architect David Rhind. It was
opened in August 1840 and a few weeks later William Branks from
Lanarkshire became the first Minister. After the great disruption
in 1843 the charge was vacant for six years as the established church
struggled to find ministers for the hundreds of deserted congregations throughout the land. In 1849 John Oswald was inducted as
the second Minister and due to his perseverance Camelon was
erected into a Parish in its own right in 1853. The life of Victorian
communities was very closely tied to that of their Parish Church
and the long ministry of the Rev John Scott (1867-1918) in many
ways symbolised the true coming of age of Camelon. He was a
leading figure not only in Camelon but in the wider Falkirk district
and it was during his time that the village, with a population of
nearly 6,000, and the town joined together in 1900 when Camelon
became part of the Burgh. Since then, the 'mariners' as the sons
and daughters of the village call themselves, have played a very full
part in the life of the larger community and the list of the institutions which serve the area from a base in Camelon is long and
impressive. There are firms like Alexander's, both bus building and
driving, and Barr's; the Mariner leisure centre and the cemetery
and crematorium; the new Sheriff Court and the Falkirk Golf Club
and, at the time of writing, even speculation that it may become
the new home of the famous Falkirk Football Club itself. Heady

days indeed for the mariners! Since 1900 no fewer than nine out of twenty four Provosts of Falkirk have come from the village.

Grangemouth

At the same time as the Forth and Clyde canal was reviving the ancient settlement of Camelon, it was bringing to birth a completely new community at the mouth of the Carron. Reporting in 1797, the Minister of Falkirk described the initiative of Sir Lawrence Dundas regarding the 'propriety of building a village and quay' at the east end of the canal:

> The place which he fixed upon for this purpose was the angle which is formed by the junction of the river Carron and the canal. They were begun to be built in the year 1777; the village is now of considerable extent and is called Grangemouth.

At first the new community was called Sealock but later it became Grange Burn Mouth from the proximity of a stream of that name which at that time meandered over the flat lands to join the Carron close to the village. Conversion to Grangemouth followed in the 1780s by which time it had a population of nearly four hundred. The provision of harbour facilities and the direct link to the rapidly expanding town of Glasgow via the canal brought swift success to the port and it soon displaced Carronshore as the principal landing place on the river. Trading vessels from all over Europe landed cargoes of grain, flax, hemp, iron and timber which were transferred in the new basins to canal lighters which carried them to factories and farms across the breadth of Scotland. In return went the coal of Lanarkshire as well as manufactured goods from foundry and mill and even the products of the new American states. In 1810 the village had a Custom's House of its own at last and no longer had to pay duties to its ancient rival Bo'ness a few miles away along the river Forth. As early as the 1790s canal boats were being built in the village including, of course, the Charlotte Dundas, from Alexander Hart's yard. The patron provided a dry-dock in 1811 and the business expanded in line with the remarkable growth of the port itself. By the late 1830s, demand had reached record levels with 750 vessels each year arriving and leaving and over 3,000

The houses in Canal Street, Grangemouth, which faced the Forth and Clyde
canal not far from its eastern harbour terminus on the River Carron.

passing through to the canal. Facilities were inadequate and a great
improvement scheme was started involving the re-direction of the
Grange burn to take it away from the harbour area to a new
meeting with the river a mile away to the east. A new dock, known
today as the 'old dock' was built, the river Carron deepened and
the major timber basin enlarged. This work was completed by '200
artificers and labourers' in 1843 by which time the population of
the village had grown to over 1,500. Even more rapid growth
followed the new developments and, less than twenty years later,
yet another, the Junction Dock, was added. These additions firmly
established Grangemouth as Scotland's principal timber import
centre and soon the storage, saw milling and distribution of red-
woods and pines from the Baltic and Canada became
Grangemouth's most important activity and the foundation of
much of its prosperity. More than a century on and the wood yards
of the port area remain of key importance to the economic wellbeing of the town with new investment reversing some of the
decline of recent years.

Long before these mid century developments the people of the
small village of Grangemouth had, like their opposite numbers in
Camelon, petitioned their Dundas patrons regarding the two special needs of every aspiring Scottish community of the period,

Charing Cross, Grangemouth, showing the short-lived Parish Church in the
distance on the left hand side.

namely a church and a school. As early as 1817 over £750 was
collected towards the provision of a church but nearly twenty years
passed before a building was erected with the support of the
Presbytery, the Minister of Falkirk and Lord Dundas, grandson of
the founder. In 1837 he, 'from due regard for the spiritual instruction of the district, erected a substantial and commodious church'
and, when the Minister and the majority of the congregation left
the established church six years later to join the new Free Church
the patron, by this time Earl of Zetland, allowed the building to be
transferred to the new church since it had never been legally
conveyed to the Church of Scotland. This caused a mighty ecclesi-
astical and legal furore but when the dust settled it was still with
the Free Church, possibly their first building in Scotland? The
newly established Parish reverted to Falkirk's control and it was not
until the 1860s that the established church had a building in the
parish—the short lived building at Charing Cross shown in the
photograph.

Education was another of the priorities and here we are told that
as early as 1797, 'Lord Dundas gives to a schoolmaster in
Grangemouth, a house to dwell in, a schoolroom and 5 pounds a
year'. In 1827 this was replaced by a new building with schoolrooms
for both boys and girls, a library, houses for the teachers and

'extensive playgrounds' which makes it quite a contrast to the dingy overcrowded buildings serving the more populous parts of the district. Again it was personal patronage of the Dundas family which ensured that the village was ahead of their rivals. This was very much in keeping with their whole approach to the design and construction of Grangemouth itself which was laid out quite deliberately in a grid pattern with streets forty feet wide and substantial dwellings built in regular fashion. The same principles were applied when the inevitable expansion of the town followed the dock extensions in the mid century. By then Grangemouth had spilled out over the canal and a whole new town was emerging on the unoccupied land to the east. But there was to be no uncontrolled sprawl as so often happened elsewhere. Careful planning again ensured that the streets were wide and well laid out and that they were filled with houses of quality each with its own garden. For 1861 this was astonishingly far sighted and the splendour of Grangemouth's 'new town' today owes much to the vision and, of course, the massive wealth of the founding fathers. At a time when it is fashionable and frequently justifiable to pillory the wealthy patrons of the Victorian era and earlier for their limited concern for the wellbeing of their communities it is refreshing to report such an outstanding example of good sense and genuine community spirit. In 1872 responsibility for municipal affairs passed from the Dundas family to a new burgh council and soon the marks of civic pride began appearing all over the prosperous town. A magnificent public park was opened in 1882 named after the Earl of Zetland and two years later he laid the foundation stone of the new Town Hall. In 1888 the handsome new Victoria Public Library was erected with the help of Andrew Carnegie's vast fortune.

Fine new churches of various denominations, public buildings and schools graced the elegant streets with Bo'ness Road, Charing Cross, Abbots Road, Talbot Street, and Ronaldshay Crescent among the most attractive. Here the well-to-do merchants and traders built high quality homes while ensuring that the working population in Marshall and Lumley Street were better served than their opposite numbers elsewhere. By the turn of the century the population was over 8000 and by then the large Carron Dock was in operation and in 1906 facilities were further improved by the opening of the Grange Dock. By then a new factor had emerged in the industrial expansion of the town.

Kerse House, the ancient seat of the families of West Kerse, Monteath, Hope and Dundas. All that remains are a few scattered stones, a garden wall and the name, the Earl's Gates.

In 1897 the Scottish Cooperative Wholesale Society established a large factory in the town making soap and glycerine. It was Grangemouth's first chemical works and was followed in 1919 by James Morton's pioneering Scottish Dyes which eventually became part of the ICI's dyestuffs division in 1928. From the huge factory which developed near the Earl of Zetland's long demolished Kerse House, that is at the Earl's Gates, came a succession of famous and money earning dyes, like the Caledon blues and Monastral greens, which secured the future for many a Grangemouth family. Four years before that Scottish Oils had opened the first Grangemouth plant to refine crude oil from the Persian Gulf and from these small beginnings the massive Grangemouth petro-chemical complex has grown to dominate all other activities in the area. It would be impossible to do justice in the space available to this particular part of Grangemouth's fascinating story; suffice to say that what became the British Petroleum refinery, processing oil brought in the through the overland pipeline from the tanker terminal at Finnart on Loch Long, attracted an array of giant chemical companies to the area anxious to convert the feedstock from the BP into the products demanded by modern societies all over the world. Since the mid 1970s the crude oil has come from deep below the waters of the North Sea and there have been a number of major new developments in the processing and manufacturing facilities.

In many ways the Refinery is the Carron of the modern era. In its scale it dwarfs all other enterprises; it is crucial to the economy not only of the district but of the whole country; it is at the forefront of new technology and, of course, its flare stacks light the night sky for miles around like those famous blast furnaces of two centuries ago. And like Carron it has inspired a steady growth in population with the inevitable demands for new housing and other facilities. Much of the empty land to the south and east of the 'new town' has disappeared under massive housing schemes and what almost amounts to a third town has grown up on the site all to briefly occupied by what was to have been a major airport in the Bowhouse area.

It was in February 1939 that Scottish Aviation announced their plans to provide central Scotland with what would be the largest airport in the country. Over 500 acres of land were secured and only five months later Grangemouth Aerodrome was officially opened by Air Marshall Viscount Trenchard. During the war Grangemouth was a centre for the training of fighter pilots and many young men, from Britain and all parts of the Commonwealth as well as Poland and Czechoslovakia, died while practising the daring manoeuvres demanded in those incredible times. Most are buried in a special part of Grandsable Cemetery, a tangible reminder of the high price we ask our children to pay when the world we have made goes awry. After the war ideas on civil aviation changed and the great plan was gradually abandoned leaving nothing now but two hanger buildings used as warehouses. Next time you drive down Inchyra Road remember that you follow in the direct path of many a Spitfire and Hurricane, and that it could so easily have been a Boeing 727 or even a Concorde. Be grateful for small mercies!

Now the grass and runways have all but vanished and the chemical industry has expanded to fill the space along with new

houses, shops and recreational facilities like the fine sports sta-
dium. Modern Grangemouth which generates so much of the
area's wealth should be the best appointed and most affluent part
of the district, and its people the most contented and self-confident. But that does not seem to be the case. The loss of separate
status in 1975 and the moving of power to Falkirk has continued
to rankle Portonians, many of whom believe that their town with
its large and growing population deserved a bigger share of the
cake and a higher priority as far as community projects were
concerned. Whatever the truth there is no doubt that a feeling of
disappointment remains and the new local government system
waiting just round the corner may offer our municipal leaders
another chance to redress the balance.

Larbert and Stenhousemuir

Like Grangemouth the twin villages of Larbert and Stenhousemuir
have a history which deserves a longer and more detailed treatment
than is possible here. Unlike Grangemouth however their origin
lies somewhere in those dark ages when the nation of Scotland was
beginning to emerge from the amalgam of Pict and Scot, Angle
and Briton. We know that the crossing point of the Carron River
was important to the Romans and that the road they constructed
from Watling Lodge on the Antonine Wall at Camelon crossed the
river by a bridge located somewhere near the present Larbert Old
Parish Church. Traces of this road were still identifiable in the
Torwood as late as the 18th century and the high and dry land
above the road and river crossing probably housed a settlement of
some kind from the earliest days. At some stage a Christian community was established in the area with a chapel which like its
counterpart in Falkirk was handed over by the Bishop of St Andrews to the Augustinian Canons as a gift in the year 1160. This
time it was the priests of Cambuskenneth rather than Holyrood
who received the 'chapels of Donypas and Lethbert', a present they
retained for almost four hundred years! Incredible as it seems, this
ancient linkage between Larbert and Dunipace survived until 1962
despite the strains of both Reformation and industrial revolution
which elsewhere tore apart the religious and social fabric of the
nation. And despite the mutual suspicion and open hostility be-

tween the two 'united parishes' which surfaced from time to time over the centuries!

Of the chapel itself we know only that around 1450 a new plain building appeared on the site of the present Kirkyard and that either before or in the immediate aftermath of the Reformation it fell into disrepair. Beyond that we have little information about the Larbert area before the 16th century but we can be sure that the turbulent relations between powerful feudal families which were the norm throughout lowland Scotland did not pass by the Larbert area. The Foresters of Garden who from the 1400s were the keepers of the valuable and strategically important royal forest of Torwood, the Bruces of Airth Castle, later also Stenhouse and Kinnaird, and the neighbouring Livingstons of Callendar shared the territory between them, at times in harmonious alliance and at others through bitter feud and conflict with much blood shed on both sides. On the slopes of the ancient wood not far from the broch already described stand the remains of Torwood Castle, the last surviving symbol of Forester power. It was built in 1566 for Sir Alexander Forester and its size and construction confirm the status

The mansion house of Stenhouse, home of the Bruce family.

of its lord and the dangerous times in which he and his family lived. The building was acquired in the 1950s by Mr Gordon Millar who has spent the last forty years or so working mostly on his own to recover and then restore the stonework of the castle. He is his own architect and mason, labourer and joiner and under his patient hand the building has been saved from the fate which has befallen many such ruins. If some parts of the restoration seem a little unusual that is a small price to pay for the love and protection poured out on this one place by a most remarkable man. It is a pity that he had not turned his mind to the ancient house of the other great family! Stenhouse the early 17th century home of the Bruces was a splendid Scottish baronial building which survived until the 1960s before being demolished despite being a listed building. It stood to the north of Carron Company who were its last owners in the vacinity of the present Lodge Drive, just yards from the site of Arthur's O'on demolished by Bruce of Stenhouse in 1743. The Bruce family also owned Kinnaird House and the present building is the third to stand on the same site—it was two of the Kinnaird Bruces who figured most prominently in the subsequent story of Larbert and Stenhousemuir.

Robert Bruce was both lawyer and churchman who had succeeded to the pulpit of John Knox himself in St Giles by 1590. At first his relations with King James VI were very close and some observers regarded him as the most powerful man in the Kingdom. Later, on a point of principle, these two determined and dogmatic men disagreed so profoundly that Bruce found himself in exile abroad and then, after some years, confined to a three-mile area around his Kinnaird home. From this base he continued to defend what he saw as the fundamentals of the protestant reformation and hundreds of people flocked to the parish to hear him preach. He restored the broken down church at Larbert and until his death in 1631 continued to attract the attention of Scotland to the little country parish. He was without doubt one of the most famous men of his generation and as 'Bruce the Covenanter' is still remembered as one of the founding fathers of the Church of Scotland.

A century later it was Robert's descendant James Bruce of Kinnaird who attained international fame as the great 'Abyssinian Traveller'. James was an intrepid adventurer who crossed the swamps, forests and deserts of Africa in the process discovering the source of the Blue Nile. His own account of these travels was thought by some to be so incredible that he was accused of fabricating the whole amazing tale. But enough people were convinced and Bruce became a living legend enjoying the favour of both royalty and Government alike. Standing over six feet, four inches tall and with a mastery of thirteen languages, it is not surprising that he impressed all the people he met—in 1773 Dr Johnson's friend Fanny Burney said that "Mr Bruce's grand air, gigantic height and forbidding brow awed everyone into silence— he is the tallest man you ever saw". Even today when men walk on the moon or sail single-handedly across the world's oceans, Bruce's two-hundred year old account remains an enthralling read. But despite the survival instinct which protected him in various foreign scrapes, he died at Kinnaird falling down the stone steps while helping a lady to her carriage! Like Robert Bruce he is buried in Larbert Old Kirkyard and the handsome cast-iron memorial he erected for his wife remains to remind the present generation of his own great prowess.

It was during James Bruce's time at Kinnaird that the greatest change in Larbert's status came about. The arrival of Carron ironworks in 1759 and its impact on the Falkirk district has already been discussed in this account and need not be repeated here. Suffice to say that it was Larbert parish which bore the immediate brunt of the great enterprise and was inevitably changed beyond recognition. The centre of gravity of the parish moved eastwards and Stenhousemuir began to grow in size and importance. Workers flocked to the village and to the neighbouring settlement of Quarrol, later Carronshore, and the social tensions began to show. In 1762 just three years after the arrival of the company the Kirk Session of Larbert recorded that there was

> a report going round of Robert Turnbull, Innkeeper at Quaroleshore, his endeavouring to seduce some young girls into the Company of some Rude people belonging to the Carron Company.

As the years passed more and more of the offenders called to answer for their misdemeaners were described as hands or wrights or even sailors working for the company. But these minor moral lapses were as nothing compared to the widespread poverty and suffering which followed the rapid expansion of iron founding and coal mining in the area. At Quarrol and Kinnaird for example, the

Larbert Old Parish Church, built in 1820 to replace an earlier building which
stood in the present graveyard shown here.

Dundas and Bruce lairds took advantage of Carron's high demands
to secure their fortunes at the expense of the wretched colliers tied
to their backbreaking labours. It was a problem that neither church
nor state seemed willing or able to tackle—in Larbert as in every
other part of Scotland as industrialisation increased the profits of
the few, their great wealth stood in sharp contrast with the misery
of those who laboured at their pits and furnaces. Instead the money
went to build or improve fine mansions for both entrepreneurs
and ancient local families and, in 1820, to a fine new church at
Larbert, designed by David Hamilton of Falkirk Steeple fame,
which has continued to grace the parish for the best part of two
centuries. As with Carron Company, the establishment of the great
Falkirk Trysts at Stenhousemuir in 1785 has already been discussed
in an earlier chapter and there is little more to add here except to
stress the further dislocation which such enormous events must
have had on a small parish and the additional work and money
which they brought into the area.

The early history of education in Larbert mirrors the experience
of most rural parishes in the days following the Reformation. At
some stage the national church's demand that a school be provided
in every parish was answered in Larbert by the establishment of
classes for children in the church building itself. Later there was

an inadequate schoolhouse built on the site of the present church halls and the Kirk Session records, which survive from 1690, report early difficulties with the heritors in providing enough money for both school and master. There was trouble too with the teachers and at least two were dismissed for immorality or being 'slothful, negligent and drunk to the detriment of the children's learning'. By the middle of the 18th century the parochial school, legally maintained by the heritors, had moved to Stenhousemuir, while the Kirk Session supported the second school in Larbert village. The money for this came from funds gathered at the church door on Sundays or from the fines levied on Larbert offenders whose regular appearances for fornication, Sabbath breaking and drunkenness ensured no shortage of cash for a worthy cause! By the 1790s there were additional schools at Kinnaird colliery and Carronshore and nearly 200 children in a rapidly expanding parish of four thousand people were attending for at least part of the week. Half a century later the numbers were more than doubled but the Minister of the parish was less than happy about the support given by some of the parents who withdrew their children at an early age because:

> colliers, moulders and others are enabled to turn their childrens labour to profitable account at the age of twelve years.

It was just one more facet of the new industrial world into which the people of Larbert and Stenhousemuir were catapulted from the beginning of the 19th century. Developments mirrored those taking place elsewhere in Falkirk district with agricultural reform followed by improvements in communications. The arrival of the Caledonian railway in the 1840s and the villages' subsequent importance as a junction provided the impetus for a wide range of new industries which appeared as the century progressed. In the late 1830s one Thomas Jones had established a timber business in Camelon where he eventually became mine host at the Union Inn. His son James worked for at time in Fairbairn's nail-works and in 1864 established his own nail-making business at Port Downie extending it to include the production of other ironware. A few years later his brother-in-law James Forbes a partner in the business joined with Major Robert Dobbie and others to create Dobbie, Forbes and Company with premises in Larbert and three years later in 1875 James Jones opened a sawmill on a site next door to the new foundry. Under the careful hand of the 'grand old man', the firm expanded to become one of Scotland's leading timber merchants with over forty different premises across the country. Everything from simple window frames by the tens of thousands to the timbers of Captain Scott's Discovery came from the Jones yard and a century and a half later the company continues to thrive.

James Jones had not completely severed his connection with the iron industry and in 1888 he formed a partnership with Dermot Campbell, the Dobbie Forbes cashier, in a foundry that still bears their names today. By then of course iron mania had swept through the whole of the Falkirk district so that by the 1890s there were twenty-five foundries with nearly nine thousand men. The village's first venture already mentioned was the Larbert Iron and Stove Works of Dobbie-Forbes which was by then employing over 200 hands. The firm are probably best remembered in the village for the handsome public hall which Major Robert Dobbie of Beechmount presented to the people in 1900 as a memorial to those lost in the wars in South Africa. The company became part of the Allied group, later Glynwed, in 1929 and, like Jones and Campbell, remains in operation today. Other celebrated enterprises followed. In order to supplement the earnings of her husband Andrew, an aerated water and confectionery salesman, a Mrs McCowan began to sell toffee from the window of her house in Stenhousemuir. It was soon more popular than the lemonade and the family took to working full-time in the sweetie business. Together Andrew and his son Robert turned Highland Cream Toffee and the famous cow into a huge national institution and established a factory in the Tryst Road. It continues today, still very much part of the fabric of village life. As late as 1927 when other ironfounders in the district were preparing to band together for survival, Robert Taylor started Muirhall Foundry, a completely new venture in the village. Judicious management and regular modernisation has ensured survival and expansion against the tide which was to sweep all but a few from the scene by the middle of the century. Indeed Larbert has been singularly successful in remaining in the iron industry with all three companies still operating at a time when the town of Falkirk, once the major centre, has none.

Another development which in its own particular way put

Larbert on the national map was the Scottish National Institution
for the Education of Imbecile Children established at a cost of
£13,000 in the 1860s on more land bought from the Stenhouse
estate. At around the same time on a nearby site the £20,000
Stirling District Lunatic Asylum opened its doors and for more than
a century the two provided through changing times for those
unfortunate enough to suffer from mental handicap or illness.
These were enormous undertakings with huge numbers of patients
living in great Victorian baronial style buildings as was the fashion
of the times. The word Royal was added during the first world war
and the RSNH was born. 'Larbert Asylum' became Bellsdyke Hospital as a new age wrestled with the difficulties of providing adequate care and security without creating a world of isolation and
despair cut off from and misunderstood by the community beyond
the high walls. The modern world continues to search for a solution and, at the time of writing, the 'care in the community'
initiative has brought about a significant reduction in the number
of patients in both hospitals. Buildings are being demolished or
sold and a modern industrial 'park' has appeared on the Bellsdyke
Road.

Back in Victorian Larbert the new captains of industry like
Dobbie and Jones built superb villas in the village which like
Polmont was distinguished by an array of fine mansions and estates.
Unlike Polmont many of them have survived to serve the community in different capacities and Kinnaird, rebuilt for the third time
in the 1890s, Torwoodhall, Beechmount, Carronvale and Car-
rongrange among others remain as a small reminder to today's
villagers of the splendour of their local heritage as well as the sweat
and struggle of the working men whose hard labour paid for most
of the grandeur.

Polmont

When the great land holdings of Abbotskerse were broken up after
the Reformation the area we know today as Polmont, Brightons,
Redding and much of the Braes area came into the hands of the
Earls, later the Dukes of Hamilton. Indeed as we noted already
when discussing the Falkirk Trysts, the present Duke and his
predecessors have Lord Polmont as a subsidiary title. The pasturage

Polmont's first church. The ruins remain in the churchyard of the present
building.

and mineral wealth of the area was exploited in the Hamilton
interest for nearly two centuries before the local residents were
strong and numerous enough to persuade the church authorities
to separate them from Falkirk in 1724 and create a new parish of
Polmont. At the time, and for decades thereafter, the village was
little more than a collection of cottages on the southern slope of
the escarpment which sweeps down to the carselands of the River
Forth. Here a new church was built and probably a school of some
kind, close by the mills and smiddy which served the farmers of the
parish. During the 19th century, long before the bridges at
Queensferry and Kincardine spanned the Forth, all traffic from
east to west and north passed along a road just to the south of
Polmont village. The Laird of Whyteside who was the feudal superior of the land agreed to allow building to take place along the
line of the road provided the new settlement was called Bennetstown—the family name! It soon became the commercial heart of
the village with small workshops, houses, schools, stores and inns.
A mile to the south, the settlement of Brightons had grown up
around a famous sandstone quarry which was in operation as early
as the 17th century. From here stone was carried by the Union
canal to help build Edinburgh's new town in the 1830s and

Millfield House, one of the finest of the Polmont mansions. It was demolished in the 1960s.

Falkirk's fine new public buildings twenty years later. The canal encouraged the development of industry and this was given further impetus by the arrival of the Edinburgh to Glasgow railway in 1842. The halt near Brightons was given the name Polmont Station and slowly but surely the original village, by then known as Old Polmont, Bennetstown, Brightons and Polmont Station began to merge into one coherent settlement.

The wealth generated by industrial success brought to Polmont the usual crop of fine mansion houses and elegant estates. There was Millfield built by John Millar, secretary of the North British Railway Company and later the home of the Stein family whose fortune came from the manufacture of refractory bricks for the expanding iron industry of the Falkirk district. And there were Polmont Park and Polmont House, mansions dating back to the late 18th century, and Polmont Bank which served as a nursing home and a hotel. All four were demolished to make way for the post-war housing and commercial developments which have so changed the character of the old village. Others like Parkhill the home of the Gray-Buchanan family survived though today it lies empty if not quite abandoned!

The growth of the village was such that by 1844 the original church was too small, 'damp, ill arranged and most inadequate' according to the Minister, and the present twin-spired building was erected in its place. The old church, now a picturesque ruin covered in ivy, stands in the kirkyard which like that of Larbert is a wonderful place to escape, for a little while, from the bustle of our modern world and find the peace and quiet of the past centuries. What a pity that the ancient graves of Falkirk Old Parish Church were cleared away in the 1960s as part of a misguided attempt to tidy up the town centre! Many of the early stones that once recorded the names of deceased parishoners now lie forgotten under the roadway to the crematorium. In loving memory indeed!

What provision was made for education in the early years of the new parish of Polmont is uncertain but by 1789 a building was provided by the heritors along with a new master, Thomas Girdwood, who remained in post for well over half a century and served as clerk to the heritors for an incredible sixty-two years! Towards the end of his time, in the 1850s, a new school was erected at a cost of £365 but by that time there were several other establishments offering education of one kind or another. The community centre on the main street was originally a school for ladies, financed by the proprietors of Polmont Park, and there were other girls' schools at Ivybank, and in the Back Row where Miss McPherson taught sewing! Perhaps the most famous educational establishment in the parish was Blairlodge Academy opened in 1843 by Robert Cunningham, a Church of Scotland minister, who also played a significant part in the Free Church breakaway in Polmont in the same year. The new school was for boy boarders and flourished under an innovative and dynamic headmaster J Cooke-Gray who took over in 1874. Modelled on the English public school system it attracted the sons of some of Scotland's wealthiest families, and inevitably, cricket and rugby were the principal sporting activities of the three hundred pupils. But there was an admirable practical strain to the curriculum and an emphasis on science which was unusual for the period. At the turn of the century Blairlodge was the largest school of its kind in Scotland and was the first to use electric lighting on such a large scale—it had nearly nine hundred bulbs at the same time as the people of Falkirk were being shown electric light as a novelty in a church bazaar! The pupils who left Blairlodge entered the privileged world of the Colonial Service, Oxford or Cambridge or into the upper echelons of the commercial world. After the death of Cooke-Gray in 1902 the school experienced financial difficulties and when it was forced to close in 1908 by an outbreak of an infectious disease, possibly measles, it never reopened. The buildings were purchased by the Prison Commissioners in 1911 and shortly afterwards opened as Scotland's first Borstal. It is now of course Polmont Young Offenders Institution.

Polmont today is a dormitory village with many new houses standing in what were once the grounds of the lost mansions. The people travel to the petrochemical complex at Grangemouth or commute daily to Glasgow and Edinburgh to work, and village life and community spirit is difficult to generate and sustain. But then Polmont is no different in this regard than many other parts of a district much changed by the demands of a very different and sometimes difficult world where a job across the road from home is now very rare and a job for life almost non-existent.

CHAPTER 12

Today and Tomorrow

The two decades since local government was reorganised and the old burgh disappeared have seen the people of Falkirk on a roller-coaster ride through decline and depression to the renewal and revived self-confidence which is evident in the area today. The decline in traditional industries continued unabated through the 1970s and, like communities throughout Britain, the spectre of high unemployment, especially among the young, was a regular visitor to the district. Successive economic crises at national level meant spending cuts in a whole range of essential services and there was little cash available to maintain the fabric of streets and buildings. Few developers were prepared to invest in new enter-prises and, as derelict foundry buildings all over the district crumbled, the very heart of the old town itself began to fall apart. Empty buildings covered in tattered posters, abandoned shops, dirty and unmended streets and the graffiti of idle hands—that was the Falkirk of the early 1980s. The people hated it but there was a resigned recognition that nothing much could be done. Municipal pride seemed at an all time low and yet there were bright spots which held out promise for a better future. For example a team of superb horticulturalists and gardeners brightened the approaches to the town and further beautified the magnificent parks by their skill and vision. Falkirk against all the odds was several times a prize winner in the Scotland and Britain in Bloom competitions and this contributed in no small measure to combating the notion that the old town was finished. But difficulties there were in abundance and it would be many years before the worst were overcome. Business confidence was at a low ebb and shoppers flocked to the grand new Thistle Centre in Stirling while Falkirk's long promised response at the Howgate became the When? gate to all but a few optimistic bairns!

New employment opportunities were desperately needed espe-cially after the double blow in the early 1980s which brought about

The pedestrianised High Street after the restoration project.

the closure of Falkirk Iron Company and then worst of all, Carron Company. The people found it difficult to believe that this colossus which had underwritten the prosperity of Falkirk for generations could possibly have failed, and many angry questions were asked by the astonished workers and their families. When the dust settled the giant was down and out and many more folk in the Falkirk district joined the growing dole queues. But recovery, or at least a kind of recovery did come again as the economic wheel turned for the district at last.

By the mid 80s the empty factory spaces and new modern units began to fill up with small business enterprises and the petrochemical

The entrance to the Howgate Centre, formerly Robert's Wynd.

complex at Grangemouth continued its remarkable expansion under the impetus of North sea oil exploitation. A group of businessmen and local politicians began a 'Think Falkirk' campaign and old animosities were buried in a communal attempt to reverse the decline. A multi-million pound programme to restore the town centre was unveiled and at long last the Howgate dream became the 'Nowgate'. The old entrance at Roberts Wynd gave way to a handsome new gateway into ultra modern and very spacious arcades of shops which soon began to attract back the business lost to the town in the years of decline. Outside, the High Street was pedestrianised and restored to a mock Victorian splendour and the narrow Wooer Street with its small shops and cafes revived an area which had for too long lain rotting and abandoned. At the east end of the High Street the ghastly Callendar Centre fell below the demolisher's hammer to the universal delight of the townspeople. In its place has come, though not without the predictable long delays and near financial disaster on the way, another new shopping area called Callendar Square. Its architecture is by popular consent more in harmony with the Edwardian and Victorian legacy

The new Callendar Square shopping centre at the east end of the High Street.

of the old town and, in this multicultural age, what if the corner tower looks more like a Cairo minaret than a Scots baronial bastion?

Elsewhere the designers abandoned the hostile lines of their predecessors and produced buildings which blended into the existing townscape. Municipal planners demanded higher standards, insisting for example on the retention of the front elevations of High Street buildings even when the premises behind them were to be demolished. The result of all this is a pleasant, even a beautiful town, much admired by visitors, where people want to shop, and dine, be entertained or even stay. Once more as in the early centuries, and again in Victoria's time, Falkirk has become the market centre of the district serving a wide area and a larger and more affluent population. And there is no shortage of new places for these welcome incomers to stay. House building seems a never ending activity in 1990s Falkirk although it is not much like the great municipal schemes which dominated in the years before and after the war. The last of these was the huge Hallglen development in the 70s. Hundreds of new houses were built on the slopes of the ancient glen in that modern style which was to fall from favour so soon afterwards. After that, central Government tightened the financial screw and this, coupled with the policy of selling council houses to sitting tenants, changed the face of new housing throughout the district.

The enforced relaxation of regulations on the use of empty sites for private development led to a rush of speculative building and on every corner, or so it seemed, a new 'mews' or 'court' appeared looking for all the world like something from the deep south of England. There were larger schemes too—exclusive and expensive developments filled the old foundry sites and finally a new village, Newcarron, rose up on the abandoned lands of Carron Company. Acres of small and quite closely packed private houses with neither kirk or school, shop nor hall—a great collection of people to be sure, but a village? Where the hammers of Mungal foundry once rent the air the sounds of the 90s are hedge-trimmers and lawn-mowers! Progress? Well maybe, but the old bairns who pass on their way to Brockville or Firs Park would be forgiven if they shake their heads and wonder. Still, no one can deny the imagination which has gone into some of the new developments. The old St Modan's Church in Cochrane Street for example has been beautifully con-verted into flats while retaining most of the character of the original building. And not far away in the Pleasance the site of the recent Roman fort excavations has also been developed with taste and style with a new Scout Hall as well as houses and flats.

For students of local history the late 1980s brought the best news of all with the agreement to restore Callendar House and use it to help tell the Falkirk story to visitors and residents alike. At the time of writing much has been achieved, enough certainly to whet the appetite for what is still to come. The hope is that the dreaded economic wheel which has so often moved at just the wrong moment, stays put until the work is completed! Callendar Park itself has become the focus for many popular community events like the regular Family Days, Highland Games and Spring Flings which attract thousands of people to the beautiful parkland setting. Indeed the District Council's entertainment department which stages these activities has done a great deal over the years to increase local participation in the arts and entertainment. For many this has meant attendance at a huge range of shows in the Town Hall and elsewhere but for others, especially young people, it has been the opportunity to participate in the Children's and Youth Theatres which have rigthy earned widespread praise across the country. For over forty years too the Falkirk and District

Arts and Civic Council has been a most powerful promoter of all kinds of activities, including the annual Falkirk Festival, a showcase for the talents of dozens of clubs and societies in the district.

Falkirk then in the 1990s seems to be a happier and more self-confident place. There are still too few jobs for young people and, despite the extensive house building, too many people unable to find a home they can afford to live in. At one time nine out of ten people in the area worked in primary work like agriculture and mining or in maufacturing industry. That figure has fallen now to around a third with the rest in the so called service sector and the trend is accelerating. The bairn of today is most likely to be an office worker, health carer, administrator or computer operator and bright new Business Parks across the district are the current magnet for such fresh jobs as there are. The site of the old College in Callendar Park houses one such venture which has brought the high-profile Child Support Agency to the town with the welcome opportunities for secure and reasonably well-paid work. In Grangemouth the Newhouse Business Park, and Central Park on the Bellsdyke Road in Larbert offer other focal points for small business growth and great efforts have been made to attract inward investment to the area. What the outcome of all these activities will be is anybody's guess. Technology is changing so fast that it would be a brave forecaster who would predict the future even with the benefit of a thousand years of historical experience. And now in 1996 local government is to be reformed once again with much power currently vested in the Region returning to where it used to be in earlier decades. Education in Falkirk for example will be directed by people in Falkirk for the first time for nearly a century!

Two hundred years ago or thereabouts the town adopted as its motto, "Touch Ane, touch a', Better Meddle wi' the Deil than the Bairns of Falkirk". It suggests a proud and pugnacious people ready to band together to protect their town and community. Such resolution will be put to the test many times in the years ahead and the future happiness and prosperity of the area may well depend on the peoples' readiness to live up to their motto. The long and rich history of the town and district suggests that they will not be found wanting.

Further Reading

A. Baird, *The Erskine Church, Falkirk* (Callander)1937

A. Bain, *Education in Stirlingshire* (U.L.P) 1965

A.I. Bowman, *Symington and the Charlotte Dundas* (Falkirk Museums) 1981

A. W. Brotchie, *The Tramways of Falkirk* (NB Traction Group) 1978

Calatria, *The Journal of the Falkirk Local History Society* (9 vols) 1991-95

R. Campbell, *Carron Company* (Oliver and Boyd)) 1961

J. Dickson et al, *Travelling Through Time, Transport in Falkirk District* (District Council Library Services) 1993

J. Fleming, *Ancient Castles and Mansions of Stirling Nobility* 1902

R. Gillespie, *Round About Falkirk* (Maclehose) 1868

A. Howson, *Camelon: Some Historical Notes* (Falkirk Museums) 1968

D. Hunter (Ed) *The Falkirk and Callendar Regality Court Book* 1638-1715(Stair Society) 1991

J. B. Johnston *Falkirk Free Church Bazaar* (Callander) 1899

R. Kier, *History of Falkirk* (Falkirk Monthly Magazine) 1827

E. Kirk, *Annals of Erskine 1737 - 1987* (Erskine Church) 1987

L. Lawson, *The Church at Falkirk* (Falkirk Old Parish Church) 1973

L. Lawson, *History of Falkirk* (Falkirk Town Council) 1975

E. Livingston, *The Livingstons of Callendar etc* (1920)

J. Love, *Schools and Schoolmasters of Falkirk* (Johnston) 1898

J. Love, *Antiquarian Notes and Queries* - 4 Volumes (Johnston) 1908 - 1928

A. Massey, *The Edinburgh and Glasgow Union Canal* (Falkirk Museums) 1983

J. R. McLuckie *The Old Kirkyard, Falkirk* (1879)

G. Murray, *Records of Falkirk Parish* - 2 Volumes (Duncan and Murray) 1988

W. F. Nicolaisen, *Scottish Place-Names* (Batsford) 1976

R. Porteous, *Grangemouth's Ancient Heritage* (Burgh of Grangemouth) 1968

R. Porteous, *Grangemouth's Modern History* (Burgh of Grangemouth) 1973

A. S. Robertson, *The Antonine Wall* (Glasgow Archaeological Society) 1979

R.C.A.H.M.S., *Stirlingshire* 2 Volumes (HMSO) 1963

I Scott and J. Ferguson, *Larbert Old Parish Church* (Larbert Old) 1993

I. Scott, *Falkirk and District Royal Infirmary 1889-1989* (Forth Valley Health Board) 1990

Essential sources for all local historical study in Scotland are the Statistical Accounts compiled by local parish ministers and published on three occasions since the last decade of the 18th century. The first or *Old Statistical Account* was edited by Sir John Sinclair and published in twenty-one volumes between 1790 and 1799. Fifty years later the exercise was repeated and the *New Statistical Account of Scotland* was the result. The parishes of Stirlingshire appeared in Volume 8 published in 1845. Over a century passed before the last survey was completed as the *Third Statistical Account of Scotland* with the counties of Stirling and Clackmannan being published in Volume XVIII in 1966. These are no dry lists of figures but fascinating essays covering an enormous range of topics - taken together they tell us a great deal about the changing face of Scotland over two centuries.

INDEX

187

190

191